# Hundred and Eight Names of Bhairava

Koushik K

**ISBN:** 9798673953631

First Printing, 2020

# Contents

# About the Hymn

This hymn is from rudrayamala tantra, the hymn is made of hundred and eight names of Vatuka Bhairava - the one who lifts us up from all kinds of troubles, dangers and calamities.

There are various dangers, troubles and calamities in this world. One can even feel sometimes that the whole life is just a struggle. Until we realize our true self. Atman which is beyond every duality (heat and coldness, brightness and darkness etc.)

We definitely need help and strength in crossing over the samsara (the cycle of birth and death) we surrender to the god in a form which we feel we can connect with easily.

Bhairava is none other than Shiva, he manifested as Bhairava the Apaduddharana to bless us and guide us through the troubles and dangers and protect us from them and make it easier for us.

Human life is very precious as it has everything required to become a seeker and realise the true self which is non-dual to supreme absolute god.

So, in times of danger, we do our part to protect ourselves from calamities both internally and externally. We pray, we seek help from the higher power. Though our ultimate aim is self-realisation, we simply seek help in handling the worldly situations which forms an obstacle in our quest of highest spiritual truth.

For those who do not have self-realisation as the aim or destination, chanting this hymn will slowly and gradually guide in that path while blessing the worldly needs which are righteous and harmless.

Bhairava not only saves us from dangers but he guides us thoroughly in our spiritual path and leads us to the experience of self-realization, he is our guru, our god our guardian. Because he is the one who grants success for the seekers say the sacred scriptures.

This hymn is very powerful and is found in Bhairavopasanadhyaya in the Upasana stabhaka which is in dharma skanda of Brihad Jyotisharnava compiled by Harikrishna Vyankatarama.

The hymn is also called Bhairava stavaraja – the king of hymns of lord Bhairava.

# Poorvapeethikaa – Introduction

Mantroddhara

मेरुपृष्ठे सुखासीनं देवदेवं त्रिलोचनम् ।
शङ्करं परिपप्रच्छ पार्वती परमेश्वरम् ॥ १॥

merupṛṣṭhe sukhāsīnaṃ devadevaṃ trilocanam |
śaṅkaraṃ paripapraccha pārvatī parameśvaram ॥ 1॥

Lord Shankara who does welfare for all the beings, he who is
the three eyed lord, (third eye represents his limitless wisdom)
the god of all gods the greatest lord and controller was asked
by goddess Parvati when the lord was happily sitting in the
mount of Meru.

He is the perfect guru hence goddess Parvati seeks his
initiation, his greatness is evident because he is devadeva –
lord of all gods, he has the nature of doing good to beings, this
shows his unconditional compassion towards all beings and
he is Parameshwara the greatest, by these qualities, you can
understand that he is the best of the gurus.

Once you find a right guru you must request him and ask him
politely your quests or doubts in the right time,

When the guru is happy, that is the right time for the disciple
to reach the guru and ask.

Lord Shiva is happily seated while mother Parvati is asking.

श्रीपार्वत्युवाच -
भगवन्सर्वधर्मज्ञ सर्वशास्त्रागमादिषु ।

आपदुद्धारणं मन्त्रं सर्वसिद्धिकरं परम् ॥ २॥

śrīpārvatyuvāca -
bhagavansarvadharmajña sarvaśāstrāgamādiṣu |
āpaduddhāraṇaṃ mantraṃ sarvasiddhikaraṃ param
॥ 2 ॥

Parvati told:
O bhagavan – one with six great qualities,

You who know all the dharma (dharma in its completeness and in its essence) it is said that the mantra which lifts us from all kinds of troubles and calamities is the way to all kinds of attainments in the sacred scriptures like agama,

सर्वेषां चैव भूतानां हितार्थं वाञ्छितं मया ।
विशेषतस्तु राज्ञां वै शान्तिपुष्टिप्रसाधनम् ॥ ३॥

sarveṣāṃ caiva bhūtānāṃ hitārtham vāñchitaṃ mayā |

viśeṣatastu rājñāṃ vai śāntipuṣṭiprasādhanam ॥ 3॥

It is wished by me (that you will teach me this) for the welfare of all the beings and especially for the kings to attain development, strength and peace. This question of hers shows her motherhood and selfless compassion for the wellbeing of all creatures.

अङ्गन्यासकरन्यासदेहन्याससमन्वितम् ।
वक्तुमर्हसि देवेश मम हर्षविवर्द्धनम् ॥ ४॥

aṅganyāsakaranyāsadehanyāsasamanvitam |

vaktumarhasi deveśa mama harṣavivarddhanam ॥ 4॥

Please initiate the mantra to me along with different nyasas (purification procedures) which will increase my happiness.

It is to be noted that feeling of happiness is the first sign for an initiation of mantra so mother says if you initiate me that will develop happiness in me.

शङ्कर उवाच -

शृणु देवि महामन्त्रमापदुद्धारहेतुकम् ।
सर्वदुःखप्रशमनं सर्वशत्रुविनाशनम् ॥ ५॥

śaṅkara uvāca -

śarṇu devi mahāmantramāpaduddhārahetukam |

sarvaduḥkhapraśamanaṃ sarvaśatruvināśanam ॥ 5॥

O goddess, listen to the mahamantra which exists for the reason of lifting (the beings) from all kinds of dangers, troubles and calamities. That which pacifies well all kinds of sorrows. That which destroys all kinds of enemies (both internal and external)

अपस्मारादि रोगानां ज्वरादीनां विशेषतः ।
नाशनं स्मृतिमात्रेण मन्त्रराजमिमं प्रिये ॥ ६॥

apasmārādi rogānāṃ jvarādīnāṃ viśeṣataḥ |

nāśanaṃ smṛtimātreṇa mantrarājamimaṃ priye ॥ 6॥

That which destroys all kinds of diseases, especially fevers, just as the effect of remembrance of mantra.

ग्रहरोगभयानां च नाशनं सुखवर्द्धनम् ।
स्नेहाद्वक्ष्यामि तं मन्त्रं सर्वसारमिमं प्रिये ॥ ७॥

graharogabhayānāṃ ca nāśanaṃ sukhavarddhanam |
snehādvakṣyāmi taṃ mantraṃ sarvasāramimaṃ priye ॥ 7॥

That which destroys grahas (those which are capable of seizing or influencing the destinies of men in a supernatural manner), diseases, illness and fear, that which increases happiness. I tell to you the essence of everything this great king of all mantras due to my love for you, O my love.

सर्वकामार्थदं पुण्यं राज्यभोगप्रदं नृणाम् ।
आपदुद्धारणमिति मन्त्रं वक्ष्याम्यशेषतः ॥ ८॥

sarvakāmārthadaṃ puṇyaṃ rājyabhogapradaṃ nṛṇām |
āpaduddhāraṇamiti mantraṃ vakṣyāmyaśeṣataḥ ॥ 8॥

This gives you every desire, that which is meritorious that which blesses us with virtue, that which gives the royal enjoyments for the beings. The mantra is called ApaduddhArana – that which lifts from dangers, I will tell to you completely.

प्रणवं पूर्वमुद्धृत्य देवी प्रणवमुद्धरेत् ।
बटुकायेति वै पश्चादापदुद्धारणाय च ॥ ९॥

कुरु द्वयं ततः पश्चाद्बटुकाय पुनः क्षिपेत् ।
देवीं प्रणवमुद्धृत्य मन्त्रोद्धारमिमं प्रिये ॥ १०॥

मन्त्रोद्धारमिदं देवी त्रैलोक्यस्यापि दुर्लभम् ।

अप्रकाश्यमिमं मन्त्रं सर्वशक्तिसमन्वितम् ॥ ११॥

pranavaṃ pūrvamuddhṛtya devī praṇavamuddharet |
baṭukāyeti vai paścādāpaduddhāraṇāya ca ॥ 9॥

kuru dvayaṃ tataḥ paścādvaṭukāya punaḥ kṣipet |
devīṃ praṇavamuddhṛtya mantroddhāramimam priye ॥ 10॥

mantroddhāramidaṃ devī trailokyasyāpi durlabham |
aprakāśyamimaṃ mantraṃ sarvaśaktisamanvitam ॥ 11॥

The code of the mantra was given in this mantra, when the code embedded in this verse is decoded the mantra is formed.

स्मरणादेव मन्त्रस्य भूतप्रेतपिशाचकाः |
विद्रवन्त्यतिभीता वै कालरुद्रादिव प्रजाः ॥ १२॥

smaraṇādeva mantrasya bhūtapretapiśācakāḥ |
vidravantyatibhītā vai kālarudrādiva prajāḥ ॥ 12॥

Just remembering this mantra makes ghost and evil spirits runs away from the devotee just like the people run away and hide on seeing the kālarudra who destroys all the worlds in the time of great dissolution.

पठेद्वा पाठयेद्वापि पूजयेद्वापि पुस्तकम् |
अग्निचौरभयं तस्य ग्रहराजभयं तथा ॥ १३॥

paṭhedvā pāṭhayedvāpi pūjayedvāpi pustakam |
agnicaurabhayaṃ tasya graharājabhayaṃ tathā ॥ 13॥

Those who recite, or teach others to recite, or even worship the book in which this mantra and the hymn is written, they are freed from fear of fire, robbers, kings and  graha - one who seizes; the power that seizes and obscures the sun and moon and causes eclipses, especially Rāhu or the ascending node; a planet (as seizing or influencing the destinies of men in a supernatural manner

न च मारिभयं किञ्चित्सर्वत्रैव सुखी भवेत् ।
आयुरारोग्यमैश्धर्यं पुत्रपौत्रादि सम्पदः ॥ १४॥

na ca māribhayaṃ kiñcitsarvatraiva sukhī bhavet |

āyurārogyamaiśvaryaṃ putrapautrādi sampadaḥ ॥ 14॥

Those who recite do not incur the fear of mass killing diseases and are happy everywhere (in all situations and in all locations) they obtain long life, great health, great wealth, sons and grandsons.

भवन्ति सततं तस्य पुस्तकस्यापि पूजनात् ।
न दारिद्र्यं न दौर्भाग्यं नापदां भयमेव च ॥ १५॥

bhavanti satataṃ tasya pustakasyāpi pūjanāt |

na dāridryaṃ na daurbhāgyaṃ nāpadāṃ bhayameva ca ॥
15॥

All the above-mentioned benefits are attained as the outcome of even worshipping the book where the mantra and stotra (hymn) is written, they don't suffer from poverty, misfortune, or any kind of danger or any kind of fear.

# Devi's Question

श्रीपार्वत्युवाच -
य एष भैरवो नाम आपदुद्धारको मतः ।
त्वया च कथितो देव भैरवःकल्प उत्तमः ॥ १६॥

śrīpārvatyuvāca -
ya eṣa bhairavo nāma āpaduddhārako mataḥ |
tvayā ca kathito deva bhairavaḥkalpa uttamaḥ || 16||

Who is this Bhairava who is titled as 'he who uplifts from dangers' you have already taught me the Bhairava Kalpa ( use of mantras and yantras for fulfilling various purposes and the method of worship of Bhairava) which is so great.

तस्य नाम सहस्राणि अयुतान्यर्बुदानि च ।
सारं समुद्धृत्य तेषां वै नामाष्टशतकं वद ॥ १७॥

tasya nāma sahasrāṇi ayutānyarbudāni ca |
sāraṃ samuddhṛtya teṣāṃ vai nāmāṣṭaśatakaṃ vada || 17||

He has thousand name hymns, even ten thousand names and millions of names, please take the essence of all such names and teach me the hundred and eight names of his.

यानि सङ्कीर्तयन्मर्त्यः सर्वदुःखविवर्जितः ।
सर्वान्कामानवाप्नोति साधकःसिद्धिमेव च ॥ १८॥

yāni saṅkīrtayanmartyaḥ sarvaduḥkhavivarjitaḥ |

sarvānkāmānavāpnoti sādhakaḥsiddhimeva ca || 18 ||

By reciting which the mortals can be freed from sorrows and attains all desires and he attains siddhi (fulfilment, fruit and the grace of the lord.

# Mantra's viniyoga

ईश्वर उवाच -
शृणु देवि प्रवक्ष्यामि भैरवस्य महात्मनः ।
आपदुद्धारकस्येदं नामाष्टशतमुत्तमम् ॥ १९॥

īśvara uvāca -
śarṇu devi pravakṣyāmi bhairavasya mahātmanaḥ ।
āpaduddhārakasyedaṃ nāmāṣṭaśatamuttamam ॥ 19॥

O goddess, I will tell you the hundred and eight names of
Bhairava the great who uplifts from all dangers


सर्वपापहरं पुण्यं सर्वापत्तिविनाशनम् ।
सर्वकामार्थदं देवि साधकानां सुखावहम् ॥ २०॥

sarvapāpaharaṃ puṇyaṃ sarvāpattivināśanam ।
sarvakāmārthadaṃ devi sādhakānāṃ sukhāvaham ॥ 20॥

The hymn rectifies all kinds of sins, it blesses us with virtue
and merit. It helps us attain all desires and all wealth, it brings
happiness to the Sadhakas (worshippers, seekers)


सर्वमङ्गलमाङ्गल्यं सर्वोपद्रवनाशनम् ।
आयुष्करं पुष्टिकरं श्रीकरं च यशस्करम् ॥ २१॥

sarvamaṅgalamaṅgalyaṃ sarvopadravanāśanam ।
āyuṣkaraṃ puṣṭikaraṃ śrīkaraṃ ca yaśaskaram ॥
21॥

That which blesses us with all fortunes and auspicious, that which destroys are troubles and pains that which gives us long life, strength, that which creates wealth and blesses us with fame and glory.

नामाष्टशतकस्यास्य छन्दोऽनुष्टुप् प्रकीर्तितः ।
बृहदारण्यको नाम ऋषिर्देवोऽथ भैरवः ॥ २२॥

nāmāṣṭaśatakasyāsya chando'nuṣṭup prakīrtitaḥ |

bṛhadāraṇyako nāma ṛṣirdevo'tha bhairavaḥ ॥ 22॥

The metre of the hymn is Anushtup, the seer is Bṛhadāraṇyaka, the deity worshipped by the hymn is Bhairava

लज्जाबीजं बीजमिति बटुकामेति शक्तिकम् ।
प्रणवः कीलकं प्रोक्तमिष्टसिद्धौ नियोजयेत् ॥ २३॥

lajjābījaṃ bījamiti baṭukāmeti śaktikam |
praṇavaḥ kīlakaṃ proktamiṣṭasiddhau niyojayet
॥ 23॥

hreem is the beejam

bhatukaya is the shakti

Om is the keelakam

This is used for the attainment of desired effects.

अष्टबाहुं त्रिनयनमिति बीजं समाहितः ।
शक्तिः ह्रीं कीलकं शेषमिष्टसिद्धौ नियोजयेत् ॥ २४॥

aṣṭabāhuṃ trinayanamiti bījaṃ samāhitaḥ |
śaktiḥ hrīṃ kīlakaṃ śeṣamiṣṭasiddhau niyojayet
|| 24||

ॐ अस्य श्रीमदापदुद्धारक-बटुकभैरवाष्टोत्तरशतनामस्तोत्रस्य
बृहदारण्यक ऋषिः । अनुष्टुप् छन्दः।
श्रीमदापदुद्धारक-वटुकभैरवो देवता ।
वं बीजम् । ह्रीं वटुकाय इति शक्तिः । प्रणवः कीलकम् ।
ममाभीष्टसिद्ध्यर्थे जपे विनियोगः ॥

ॐ asya śrīmadāpaduddhāraka-
baṭukabhairavāṣṭottaraśatanāmastotrasya
bṛhadāraṇyaka ṛṣiḥ | anuṣṭup chandaḥ|
śrīmadāpaduddhāraka-vaṭukabhairavo devatā |
vaṃ bījam | hrīṃ vaṭukāya iti śaktiḥ | praṇavaḥ kīlakam |
mamābhīṣṭasiddhyarthe jape viniyogaḥ ||

for this hymn of hundred and eight names of
śrīmadāpaduddhāraka-baṭukabhairava

bṛhadāraṇyaka is the seer
anuṣṭup is the metre
śrīmadāpaduddhāraka-baṭukabhairava is the deity
vaṃ is the beejam (seed mantra)
hrīṃ vaṭukāya is shakti (power mantra)
Om is the keelaka (key mantra)

It is used for the fulfilment of my desires.

# Importance of Nyāsa

Nyasa is the procedure of touching different parts of the body while chanting the different names or different mantras of the god while meditating upon the god.

This is done for the purification of our mind, words, body and deed.

By doing the nyasa we realise that every part of our body is god, mind is god, words we utter (the mantras) is also god. We become one with god and then we start meditating upon the prescribed appearance of god and start worshipping him by chanting or reciting the mantra and stotra (hymn)

Nyasa in combination with mantra japa (chanting) helps in connecting with god and god realisation.

# Rushayadi Nyāsa



॥ ऋष्यादि न्यासः ॥

श्रीबृहदारण्यकऋषये नमः (शिरसि)।
अनुष्टप् छन्दसे नमः (मुखे)।
श्रीबटुकभैरव देवतायै नमः (हृदये)।
ॐ बं बीजाय नमः (गुह्ये)।
ॐ ह्रीं वटुकायेति शक्तये नमः पादयोः ।
ॐ कीलकाय नमः (नाभौ)।
विनियोगाय नमः सर्वाङ्गे ।
॥ इति ऋष्यादि न्यासः ॥

॥ ṛṣyādi nyāsaḥ ॥

śrībṛhadāraṇyakarṣaye namaḥ (śirasi)। (head)
anuṣṭap chandase namaḥ (mukhe)। (mouth)
śrībaṭukabhairava devatāyai namaḥ (hṛdaye)। (heart)
ॐ vaṃ bījāya namaḥ (guhye)। (private organ)
ॐ hrīṃ vaṭukāyeti śaktaye namaḥ pādayoḥ । (feet)
ॐ kīlakāya namaḥ (nābhau)।    (navel)
viniyogāya namaḥ sarvāṅge । (all over the body)
॥ iti ṛṣyādi nyāsaḥ ॥

# Kara Nyāsa

॥ अथ करन्यासः ॥

ॐ ह्रां वां ईशानाय नमः अङ्गुष्ठाभ्यां नमः ।
ॐ ह्रीं वीं तत्पुरुषाय नमः तर्जनीभ्यां नमः ।
ॐ ह्रूं वूं अघोराय नमः मध्यमाभ्यां नमः ।
ॐ ह्रैं वैं वामदेवाय नमः अनामिकाभ्यां नमः ।
ॐ ह्रौं वौं सद्योजाताय नमः कनिष्ठिकाभ्यां वमः ।
ॐ ह्रः वः पञ्चवक्त्राय महादेवाय नमः करतलकरपृष्ठाभ्यां नमः ।
॥ इति करन्यासः ॥


॥ atha karanyāsaḥ ॥


ॐ hrāṃ vāṃ īśānāya namaḥ aṅguṣṭhābhyāṃ namaḥ ।
(thumb fingers)
ॐ hrīṃ vīṃ tatpuruṣāya namaḥ tarjanībhyāṃ namaḥ ।
(index fingers)
ॐ hrūṃ vūṃ aghorāya namaḥ madhyamābhyāṃ namaḥ ।
(ring fingers)
ॐ hraiṃ vaiṃ vāmadevāya namaḥ anāmikābhyāṃ namaḥ
। (middle fingers)
ॐ hrauṃ vauṃ sadyojātāya namaḥ kaniṣṭhikābhyāṃ
vamaḥ । (little fingers)

ॐ hraḥ vaḥ pañcavaktrāya mahādevāya namaḥ karatalakarapṛṣṭhābhyāṁ namaḥ I (front and back of the hand)

17

# Hrudayadi nyasa

‖ अथ हृदयादि न्यासः ‖

ॐ ह्रां वां ईशानाय नमः हृदयाय नमः ।
ॐ ह्रीं वीं तत्पुरुषाय नमः शिरसे स्वाहा ।
ॐ हूं वूं अघोराय नमः शिखायै वषट् ।
ॐ ह्रैं वैं वामदेवाय नमः कवचाय हुम् ।
ॐ ह्रौं वौं सद्योजाताय नमः नेत्रत्रयाय वौषट् ।
ॐ हः वः पञ्चवक्त्राय महादेवाय नमः अस्त्राय फट् ।
‖ इति हृदयादि न्यासः ‖

‖ atha hṛdayādi nyāsaḥ ‖

ॐ hrāṃ vāṃ īśānāya namaḥ hṛdayāya namaḥ । (heart)
ॐ hrīṃ vīṃ tatpuruṣāya namaḥ śirase svāhā । (head)
ॐ hrūṃ vūṃ aghorāya namaḥ śikhāyai vaṣaṭ । (crest)
ॐ hraiṃ vaiṃ vāmadevāya namaḥ kavacāya hum । (armour)
ॐ hrauṃ vauṃ sadyojātāya namaḥ netratrayāya vauṣaṭ ।
(eyes)
ॐ hraḥ vaḥ pañcavaktrāya mahādevāya namaḥ astrāya phaṭ ।
(weapon)
‖ iti hṛdayādi nyāsaḥ ‖

# Deha Nyāsa

अथ देहन्यासः ।
भैरवं मूर्ध्नि विन्यस्य ललाटे भीमदर्शनम् ।
नेत्रयोर्भूतहननं सारमेयानुगं भ्रुवोः ॥ २५॥

कर्णयोर्भूतनाथं च प्रेतबाहुं कपोलयोः ।
नासौष्ठयोश्चैव तथा भस्माङ्गं सर्पविभूषणम् ॥ २६॥

अनादिनाथं च शक्तिहस्तं गले न्यसेत् ।
स्कन्धयोर्दैत्यशमनं वाह्वोरतुलतेजसः ॥ २७॥

पाण्योः कपालिनं न्यस्य हृदये मुण्डमालिनम् ।
शान्तं वक्षस्थले न्यस्य स्तनयोः कामचारिणम् ॥ २८॥

उदरे च सदा तुष्टं क्षेत्रेशं पार्श्वयोस्तथा ।
क्षेत्रपालं पृष्ठदेशे क्षेत्रज्ञं नाभिदेशके ॥ २९॥

पापौघनाशनं कट्यां बटुकं लिङ्गदेशके ।
गुदे रक्षाकरं न्यस्येत्तथोर्वोर्रक्तलोचनम् ॥ ३०॥

जानुनोर्घुर्घुरारावं जङ्घयो रक्तपाणिनम् ।
गुल्फयोः पादुकासिद्धं पादपृष्ठे सुरेश्वरम् ॥ ३१॥

आपादमस्तकं चैव आपदुद्धारकं तथा ।

bhairavaṃ mūrdhni vinyasya lalāṭe bhīmadarśanam |
netrayorbhūtahananaṃ sārameyānugaṃ bhruvoḥ ‖ 25‖

karṇayorbhūtanātham ca pretabāhum kapolayoḥ |
nāsauṣṭhayościava tathā bhasmāṅgam sarpavibhūṣaṇam ||
26 ||

anādinātham āsye ca śaktihastam gale nyaset |
skandhayordaityaśamanam bāhvoratulatejasaḥ || 27 ||

pāṇyoḥ kapālinam nyasya hṛdaye muṇḍamālinam |
śāntam vakṣasthale nyasya stanayoḥ kāmacāriṇam || 28 ||

udare ca sadā tuṣṭam kṣetreśam pārśvayostathā |
kṣetrapālam pṛṣṭhadeśe kṣetrajñam nābhideśake || 29 ||

pāpaughanāśanam kaṭyām baṭukam liṅgadeśake |
gude rakṣākaram nyasyettathorvorraktalocanam || 30 ||

jānunorghurghurārāvam jaṅghayo raktapāṇinam |
gulphayoḥ pādukāsiddham pādapṛṣṭhe sureśvaram || 31 ||

āpādamastakam caiva āpaduddhārakam tathā |

bhairava (head)
bhīmadarśana (forehead)
bhūtahanana (both the eyes)
sārameyānuga (eye brows)
bhūtanātha (in the ears)
pretabāhu (in both the cheeks)
bhasmāṅga (nose)
sarpavibhūṣaṇa (lips)

anādinātha (face)
śaktihastaṃ (neck)
daityaśamana (shoulders)
atulateja (arms)
kapālin (hands)
muṇḍamālin (heart)
śānta (chest)
kāmacāriṇ (breasts)
sadā tuṣṭa (Stomach)
kṣetreśa (the region of the ribs or the part of the body below
the armpit; the side,)
kṣetrapāla (back)
kṣetrajña (navel)(
pāpaughanāśana (hip)
baṭuka (genital organ)
rakṣākara (anus)
raktalocana (thighs)
ghurghurārāva (knees)
raktapāṇin (Shanks)
pādukāsiddha (ankles)
sureśvara (back side of feet – upper side of feet)
āpaduddhāraka (from head to feet)

# DigNyāsa

पूर्वे डमरुहस्तं च दक्षिणे दण्डधारिणम् ॥ ३२॥

खड्गहस्तं पश्चिमायां घण्टावादिनमुत्तरे ।
आग्नेय्यामग्निवर्णं च नैरृत्ये च दिगम्बरम् ॥ ३३॥

वायव्यां सर्वभूतस्थमैशान्ये चाष्टसिद्धिदम् ।
ऊर्ध्वं खेचारिणं न्यस्य पाताले रौद्ररूपिणम् ॥ ३४॥

pūrve ḍamaruhastaṃ ca dakṣiṇe daṇḍadhāriṇam ॥ 32॥

khaḍgahastaṃ paścimāyāṃ ghaṇṭāvādinamuttare ।
āgneyyāmagnivarṇaṃ ca nairṛtye ca digambaram ॥ 33॥

vāyavyāṃ sarvabhūtasthamaiśānye cāṣṭasiddhidam ।
ūrdhvaṃ khecāriṇaṃ nyasya pātāle raudrarūpiṇam ॥ 34॥

ḍamaruhasta (east)
dakṣiṇe (south)
khaḍgahasta (west)
ghaṇṭāvādin (north)
agnivarṇa (south east)
digambara (south west)
sarvabhūtastha (north west)
aṣṭasiddhida (north east)
khecāriṇ (zenith - up)
raudrarūpiṇ (nadir - down)

# Nāma Karanyāsa

एवं विन्यस्य स्वदेहस्य षडङ्गेषु ततो न्यसेत् ।
रुद्रं अङ्गुष्ठयोर्न्यस्य तर्जन्योश्च दिवाकरम् ॥ ३५॥

शिवं मध्यमयोर्न्यस्य अनामिकायां त्रिशूलिनम् ।
ब्रह्माणं तु कनिष्ठिक्यां स्तनयोस्त्रिपुरान्तकम् ॥ ३६॥

मांसासिनं कराग्रे तु करपृष्ठे दिगम्बरम् ।

evaṃ vinyasya svadehasya ṣaḍaṅgeṣu tato nyaset |
rudraṃ aṅguṣṭhayornyasya tarjanyośca divākaram ॥ 35॥

śivaṃ madhyamayornyasya anāmikāyāṃ triśūlinam |
brahmāṇam tu kaniṣṭhikyāṃ stanayostripurāntakam ॥ 36॥
māṃsāsinaṃ karāgre tu karapṛṣṭhe digambaram |

rudra (thumb fingers)
divākaram (index fingers)
śivaṃ (ring finger)
triśūlin (middle finger)
brahma (little finger)
māṃsāsin (palm)
digambara (back of the hand)

# Nāmāṅga Nyāsa

अथ नामाङ्गन्यासः ।
हृदये भूतनाथाय आदिनाथाय मूर्द्धनि ॥ ३७॥

आनन्दपादपूर्वाय नाथाय च शिखासु च ।
सिद्धसाबरनाथाय कवचं विन्यसेत्ततः ॥ ३८॥

सहजानन्दनाथाय न्यसेन्नेत्रत्रयेषु च ।
परमानन्दनाथाय अस्त्रं चैव प्रयोजयेत् ॥ ३९॥

एवं न्यासविधिं कृत्वा यथावत्तदनन्तरम् ।

atha nāmāṅganyāsaḥ |
hṛdaye bhūtanāthāya ādināthāya mūrddhani ॥ 37॥

ānandapādapūrvāya nāthāya ca śikhāsu ca |
siddhasābaranāthāya kavacaṃ vinyasettataḥ ॥ 38॥

sahajānandanāthāya nyasennetratrayeṣu ca |
paramānandanāthāya astraṃ caiva prayojayet ॥ 39॥

evaṃ nyāsavidhiṃ kṛtvā yathāvattadanantaram |

bhūtanāthāya namah (heart)
ādināthāya namah (head)
ānanda nāthāya namah (crest)
siddhasābaranāthāya  namah (armour)

sahajānandanāthāya (in three eyes – two eyes and point
between the eye brows)
paramānandanāthāya namah (celestial weapon)

25

# Dhyānam

तस्य ध्यानं प्रवक्ष्यामि यथा ध्यात्वा पठेन्नरः ॥ ४०॥

शुद्धस्फटिकसङ्काशं सहस्रादित्यवर्चसम् ।
नीलजीमूतसङ्काशं नीलाञ्जनसमप्रभम् ॥

अष्टबाहुं त्रिनयनं चतुर्बाहुं द्विबाहुकम् ।
दशबाहुमथोग्रं च दिव्याम्बरपरिग्रहम् ॥

दंष्ट्राकरालवदनं नूपुरारावसङ्कुलम् ।
भुजङ्गमेखलं देवमग्निवर्णं शिरोरुहम् ॥

दिगम्बरकुमारेशं बटुकाख्यं महाबलम् ।
खट्वाङ्गमसिपाशं च शूलं दक्षिणभागतः ॥

डमरुं च कपालं च वरदं भुजगं तथा ।
आत्मवर्णसमोपेतं सारमेयसमन्वितम् ॥

॥ इति ध्यानम् ॥


śuddhasphaṭikasaṅkāśaṃ sahasrādityavarcasam |
nīlajīmūtasaṅkāśaṃ nīlāñjanasamaprabham ||

aṣṭabāhuṃ trinayanaṃ caturbāhuṃ dvibāhukam |
daśabāhumathograṃ ca divyāmbaraparigraham ||

daṃṣṭrākarālavadanaṃ nūpurārāvasaṅkulam |

bhujaṅgamekhalaṃ devamagnivarṇaṃ śiroruham ||

digambarakumāreśaṃ baṭukākhyaṃ mahābalam |
khaṭvāṅgamasipāśaṃ ca śūlaṃ dakṣiṇabhāgataḥ ||

ḍamaruṃ ca kapālaṃ ca varadaṃ bhujagaṃ tathā |
ātmavarṇasamopetaṃ sārameyasamanvitam ||

I will describe the verses of contemplation of lord bhairava which guides a devotee how to visualize.

He is white as clear crystal, dark as the blue mountain. Has eight hands, four hands or two hands, he has fierce fanglike teeth, he is shining with anklets that make tinkling sounds. He has a snake as his waist-belt, he who has long locks of hair which appears like fire. He has directions as his cloth (he who is naked) he is the lord of kumārīs. He is called vatuka, he is very strong. He holds khadvanga (a weapon which looks like a skull which is placed upon a staff.), sword, lasso and trident in for of his right hands. Drum, skull, gesture of wish giving and snake in four of his left hands, he is in the complexion of fire, he is accompanied by a wild dog, after meditating upon him in such form, once should recite the hymn, and will attain all the desires.

# Sattvica Dhyānam

मन्त्रमहार्णवे सात्त्विकध्यानम् -
वन्दे बालं स्फटिकसदृशं कुण्डलोद्भासिवक्त्रं
दिव्याकल्पैर्नवमणिमयैः किङ्किणीनूपुराढ्यैः ।
दीप्ताकारं विशदवदनं सुप्रसन्नं त्रिनेत्रं
हस्ताग्राभ्यां वटुकमनिशं शूलदण्डौ दधानम् ॥

vande bālaṃ sphaṭikasadṛśaṃ kuṇḍalodbhāsivaktraṃ
divyākalpairnavamaṇimayaiḥ kiṅkiṇīnūpurāḍhyaiḥ |
dīptākāraṃ viśadavadanaṃ suprasannaṃ trinetraṃ
hastāgrābhyāṃ vaṭukamaniśaṃ śūladaṇḍau dadhānam ||

I bow and salute to the one who is a little kid, who is shining like a clear crystal in colour. He whose ears are adorned by the ear ornaments kundela which reflect in his cheeks. He is also adorned with the divine ornaments made of nine precious gems, wears a girdle of small bells on his hip, an anklet. He is shining with all those ornaments, and is very happy, has three eyes, he is holding trident and staff in his hands. He looks like a vatu. (A learner of the Vedas who is maintaining celibacy and following certain vows)

# Rajasa Dhyanam

मन्त्रमहार्णवे राजसध्यानम् -
उद्यद्भास्करसन्निभं त्रिनयनं रक्ताङ्गरागस्रजं
स्मेरास्यं वरदं कपालमभयं शूलं दधानं करैः ॥

नीलग्रीवमुदारभूषणयुतं शीतांशुखण्डोज्ज्वलं
बन्धूकारुणवाससं भयहरं देवं सदा भावये ॥ २॥

udyadbhāskarasannibham trinayanam
raktāṅgarāgasrajam
smerāsyam varadam kapālamabhayam
śūlam dadhānam karaiḥ ॥

nīlagrīvamudārabhūṣaṇayutam śītāmśukhaṇḍojjvalam
bandhūkāruṇavāsasam bhayaharam devam sadā bhāvaye ॥
2॥

He looks like the rising sun, he has three eyes, has applied red
sandal paste on him, wears garlands of red flowers , he has a
beautiful smile on his face, he shows the gesture of wish
giving, holds a skull, gesture of protection and trident in four
of his hands, his neck is blue, he is adorned with may
ornaments , he bears a moon on his crest. He is covered by a
cloth which is red like the Pentapetes Phœnicea flower. He
rectifies fear, I always visualize the god.

# Tamasa dhyanam

मन्त्रमहार्णवे तामसध्यानम् -
ध्यायेन्नीलाद्रिकान्तिं शशिशकलधरं मुण्डमालं महेशं
दिग्वस्त्रं पिङ्गलाक्षं डमरुमथ सृणिं खड्गपाशाभयानि ॥

नागं घण्टां कपालं करसरसिरुहैर्बिभ्रतं भीमदंष्ट्रं,
दिव्याकल्पं त्रिनेत्रं मणिमयविलसत्किङ्किणीनूपुराढ्यम् ॥ ३॥


॥ इति ध्यानत्रयम् ॥


mantramahārṇave tāmasadhyānam -
dhyāyennīlādrikāntiṃ śaśiśakaladharaṃ
muṇḍamālaṃ maheśaṃ
digvastraṃ piṅgalākṣaṃ ḍamarumatha sṛṇiṃ
khaḍgapāśābhayāni ॥

nāgaṃ ghaṇṭāṃ kapālaṃ
karasarasiruhairbibhrataṃ bhīmadaṃṣṭraṃ,
divyākalpaṃ trinetraṃ
maṇimayavilasatkiṅkiṇīnūpurāḍhyam ॥ 3॥


॥ iti dhyānatrayam ॥


He who has the radiance of the blue mountain, who bears a
piece of moon on his crest, wears a garland of heads, he who
is the greatest of the lords, he who has the directions as his
covering (cloth), he who has reddish-brown hair, he holds a
small drum, elephant goad, sword, lasso, gesture of
protection, serpent, bell, skull, in his eight lotus like hands, he

has fierce teeth, m he is decorated with divine ornaments, has three eyes, he wears a girdle of small bells on his hip and an anklet.

# Benefits of the three kinds of Dhyana

सात्त्विकं ध्यानमाख्यातञ्चतुर्वर्गफलप्रदम् ।
राजसं कार्यशुभदं तामसं शत्रुनाशनम् ॥ १॥

ध्यात्वा जपेत्सुसंहृष्टः सर्वान्कामानवाप्नुयात् ।
आयुरारोग्यमैश्वर्यं सिद्ध्यर्थं विनियोजयेत् ॥ २॥

sāttvikaṃ dhyānamākhyātañcaturvargaphalapradam |
rājasaṃ kāryaśubhadaṃ tāmasaṃ śatrunāśanam ॥ 1॥

dhyātvā japetsusaṃhṛṣṭaḥ sarvānkāmānavāpnuyāt |
āyurārogyamaiśvaryaṃ siddhyarthaṃ viniyojayet ॥ 2॥


sāttvika dhyāna (visualization) of bhairava helps us attain all four benefits of life. Dharma (righteousness) artha (wealth) kaama (desire) and moksha (ultimate liberation)

rājasa dhyāna (visualization) helps in attaining success in various deeds.

Tāmasa dhyāna (visualization) is done to destroy the enemies.

After doing the visualization, one must chat the hymn and by that one can attain all the desired benefits. ;one can get long life, health, wealth and all other attainments by reciting the hymn,

# Viniyoga of stotra

विनियोगः

ॐ अस्य श्रीबटुकभैरवनामाष्टशतकस्य आपदुद्धारणस्तोत्रमन्त्रस्य,
बृहदारण्यको नाम ऋषिः, श्रीबटुकभैरवो देवता, अनुष्टुप् छन्दः,
ह्रीं बीजम्, बटुकायेति शक्तिः, प्रणवः कीलकं, अभीष्टतां सिद्ध्यिर्थे
जपे विनियोगः ॥ ह्रीं ह्रौं नमः शिवाय इति नमस्कार मन्त्रः ॥

viniyogaḥ
ॐ asya śrībaṭukabhairavanāmāṣṭaśatakasya
āpaduddhāraṇastotramantrasya,
bṛhadāraṇyako nāma ṛṣiḥ, śrībaṭukabhairavo
devatā, anuṣṭup chandaḥ,
hrīṃ bījam, vaṭukāyeti śaktiḥ, praṇavaḥ
kīlakaṃ, abhīṣṭatāṃ siddhyirthe
jape viniyogaḥ ॥ hrīṃ hrauṃ namaḥ śivāya iti

namaskāra mantraḥ ॥

for the hundred and eight names of vatuka bhairava

seer is bṛhadāraṇyaka
metre is anuṣṭup
śrībaṭukabhairava is the deity
hrīṃ is the seed mantra
vaṭukāya is the power mantra
Om is the key mantra.
hrīṃ hrauṃ namaḥ śivāya is the salutation mantra

it is recited for the fulfilment of all desired benefits.

॥ अथ ध्यानम् ॥

करकलितकपालः कुण्डली दण्डपाणिः
तरुणतिमिरनीलो व्यालयज्ञोपवीती ।
क्रतुसमयसपर्याविघ्नविच्छिप्तिहेतुः
जयति वटुकनाथः सिद्धिदः साधकानाम् ॥

karakalitakapālaḥ kuṇḍalī daṇḍapāṇiḥ
taruṇatimiranīlo vyālayajñopavītī |
kratusamayasaparyāvighnavicchiptihetuḥ
jayati vaṭukanāthaḥ siddhidaḥ sādhakānām ||

He who holds a skull and staff in his hands, he who wears a kundala ornament on his ears, he who is dark in complexion like the evening darkness, he who has a snake as his sacred thread, that vaṭukanātha the lord of the vatus is excelling. He who is the giver of fruits to the worshippers.

॥ मूलमन्त्रः ॥

ॐ ह्रीं बटुकायापदुद्धारणाय कुरु कुरु बटुकाय ह्रीं ॐ

ॐ hrīṃ baṭukāyāpaduddhāraṇāya kuru kuru
baṭukāya hrīṃ ॐ

You can chant this mantra for at least hundred and eight times
before chanting the hundred and eight names hymn.

# Om bhairavāya namaḥ

Bhairava in general means formidable, awful, horrible, terrific, terrible, horrid

lord of terror

rava means cry, roar yell etc.

The word bhai – indicates fear or terror, bhairava is the one whose roar is terrific and fierce.

Shankara in his kala bhairavashtakam say

attahAsa Binna padmajAndakOSa santatim

He whose laughter destroys a multitude of brahmandas. If his loud laughter can do this much of destruction, then let us imagine how much destruction can his war cry cause. Hence, he is called bhairava.

# Om bhūtanāthāya namaḥ ।

bhūta means elements, living beings, the bhuta ghanas of lord Shiva.

भूतग्रामानां नाथः भूथनाथः

तैर्नाथ्यते तैर्याच्यते तानुपतपति तेषामीष्टे शाश्तीति वा नाथः

bhūtagrāmānāṃ nāthaḥ bhūthanāthaḥ

tairnāthyate tairyācyate tānupatapati teṣāmiṣṭe śāśtīti vā nāthaḥ

He is requested by them , begged to by them , he orders them, he is worshipped by them hence he is nātha.

nātha – protector, patron, master, leader, ruler, lord

Lord bhairava is the lord of all five elements, all the living beings and the leader of the ghanas and hence he is called bhūtanātha

He is not only the lord of bhutas but he protects them, he maintains balance and bestows upon the living beings the fruit of karma.

# Om bhūtātmane namaḥ

भूतानामात्मान्तर्यामीति भूतात्मा

एष त आत्मान्तर्याम्यमृतः
   - इति श्रुतेः

bhūtānāmātmāntaryāmīti bhūtātmā

eṣa ta ātmāntaryāmyamṛtaḥ
-       iti śruteḥ

He who resides in every butha

He is non-different from Shiva so we can understand that he is the ashtamurthy – who resides in the five great elements, the sun, moon and yajamana (soul)

He is the atman 'true self' of all the beings.

There is nothing which is different from him or beyond him, it is only he who has pervaded the whole world.

# Om bhūtabhāvanāya namaḥ

भूतानि भावयति जनयति वर्धयतीति वा भूतभावनः

bhūtāni bhāvayati janayati vardhayatīti vā bhūtabhāvanaḥ

He who creates, develops the beings.

Only because of the existence of brahman, everything else seems like existing. (i.e.) everything is like the reflection of brahman; hence he is the prime reason and the only reason for existence and development of the beings.

# Om kṣetrajñāya namaḥ

क्षेत्रं शरीरं जानातीति क्षेत्रज्ञः

kṣetraṃ śarīraṃ jānātīti kṣetrajñaḥ

he who knows well about the body

क्षेत्राणि हि शरीराणि
बीजे चापि शुभाशुभं
तानि वेति स योगात्मा
ततः क्षेत्रज्ञ उच्यते

प्रकृतेश्च विकाराणां द्रष्टारमगुणान्वितं
क्षेत्रज्ञमाहुर्जीवं तु कर्तारं गुणसंभृतं
इति महाभारते शान्तिपर्वणि

kṣetrāṇi hi śarīrāṇi
bīje cāpi śubhāśubhaṃ
tāni vetti sa yogātmā
tataḥ kṣetrajña ucyate

prakṛteśca vikārāṇāṃ draṣṭāramaguṇānvitaṃ
kśetragyamāhurjīvaṃ tu kartāraṃ guṇasaṃbhṛtaṃ
iti mahābhārate śāntiparvaṇi

The bodies are called kshetras, shubha and ashubha karma are
the seeds. He who knows and understands the body and the
good and bad karma, is called kṣetrajña.

महाभूतान्यहंकारो बुद्धिरव्यक्तमेवच
इन्द्रियाणि दशंचैक पञ्चचेन्द्रियगोचराः
इच्छा द्वेषः सुखं दुःखं संघातः चेतना धृतिः
एतत् क्षेत्रं समासेन सविकारमुदाहृतं

उक्तप्रकारमात्मत्वेन जानातीति क्षेत्रज्ञः

mahābhūtānyahaṃkāro buddhiravyaktamevaca
indriyāṇi daśaṃcaika pañcacendriyagocarāḥ
icchā dveṣaḥ sukhaṃ duḥkhaṃ saṃghātaḥ cetanā dhṛtiḥ
etat kṣetraṃ samāsena savikāramudāhṛtaṃ

uktaprakāramātmatvena jānātīti kṣetrajñaḥ

The five great elements the feeling of I, intellect, unmanifest, the ten sense organs and mind, five sensory objects, desire, hatred, happiness, sorrow, association, consciousness, steadiness all these are collectively called as kshetra.

He who knows this as the seer the perceiver

क्षेत्रज्ञः संकल्पाध्यवसायाभिमानी लिङ्ग इति श्रुतिः

kṣetrajñaḥ saṃkalpādhyavasāyābhimānī liṅga iti śrutiḥ

# Om kṣetrapālāya namaḥ

He is the one who protects the kshetras, gaurds the kshetras.

Kshetras are holy places or shrines, regions of land

Our body is also called kshetra

He protects all these kinds of kshetras and hence he is kṣetrapāla.

# Om kṣetradāya namaḥ

He is the one who gives us the kshetra. Only he has gifted us this body for us to do your duties and deeds. One can only give what he owns, this means he owns our body and has given it to us for a purpose.

He is the one who gives lands to his devotees

# Om kṣatriyāya namaḥ।

क्षता त्रायते इति क्षत्रियः

kṣatā trāyate iti kṣatriyaḥ

he who protects us by hurting, punishing or destroying.

He is the giver of fruit to our karma

Acharya shankara also says loka puNya pApa SoDakaM viBum" in his kAlaBairavAStakaM

The lord punishes us for our bad karma for purifying us, teaching us life lessons through the punishments, he maintains the divine order. His punishments are like those given by a loving father. The intension is our welfare and making us stand in the right path. (righteous path)

# Om viraje namaḥ ।

The consciousness which perceives collections or aggregates, the supreme being, he who is in the form of the universe, universal consciousness

# Om śmaśānavāsine namaḥ

He who lives in the cremation ground

The shasrAra chakra is also called the great cremation ground. The lord resides in that top most chakra and hence he is called śmaśāna vāsin. The yogic state of mahA samADi is the mahASmaSAna because there is nothing else left, no thoughts nor action.

He lives in the cremation ground out of his ultimate compassion, he controls and calms down the ghostly beings, there is another great explanation given by great saints,

Some go to temple, some don't, some go to places where noble deeds are done and participate, cremation ground is where every being comes (i.e.) death is common and unavoidable for every being, hence he lives there to show that he wants every being to come to him, connect with him in some way and experience him.

# Om māṃsāśine namaḥ ।

47

He who eats meat.

He is the embodiment of time and death, he is the destroyer, only because of his will our body is destroyed, i.e.) we face death. That is indicated by his meat eating. Death happens in time and because of time, whatsoever may be the cause of death, all that is born is to be dead one day or the other and he is the one who controls that.

# Om karparāśine namaḥ

He who eats in a skull cup / skull vessel

Karpara also means a beggar's bowl.

He uses it as his eating vessel.

That is a part of is conduct to beg and eat as he is in the form of a brahmachāri – he who practices sacred study as an unmarried student.

# Om smarāṃtakāya namaḥ।

He who has destroyed smara (he who emerged from the mind of brahma the creator) the god of love, lust and attraction.

The lord has defeated desire and guide his devotees to defeat desire, lust, attachment etc. he is the greatest of the yogis. He helps us to attain the wisdom which frees us from attachment.

# Om raktapāya namaḥ

He who drinks blood.

He who drinks the rakti (desire and attachment) from the minds of the yogis and save them from desires.

He who protects the ratki (love and affection) we have towards god. (Shiva)

# Om pānapāya namaḥ

He who drinks the divine wine.

Wine is the symbol of divine eternal bliss, the amrta. The wisdom of the self and enjoyment of the consciousness is the intoxication says the sacred scriptures.

# Om siddhāya namaḥ।

नित्यनिष्पन्नरूपत्वाद् सिद्धः

nityaniṣpannarūpatvād siddhaḥ

For accomplishing anything, we have a mean a method to follow and then we accomplish it either temporarily or permanently. He the brahman ( the ultimate supreme godhood who is non dual to our true self) is already accomplished and we needed do anything to accomplish him but just realize the experience of brahman (atman) that is already being experienced. All the methods and means of sadhana to attain god are only methods to help us gain that knowledge to realize that we already have him and we only have him and nothing other than him exists.

अनन्याधीन सिद्धित्वात् सिद्धः

ananyādhīna siddhitvāt siddhaḥ

His success and attainment don't depend on any other superior or any other factor, hence he is called siddha. He has control over his will and he can attain anything he wishes to. His power and authority are limitless. He is not controlled by any other.

स्वप्रकाशत्वात् सिद्धः

svaprakāśatvāt siddhaḥ

He is self-luminous. He doesn't depend on any other support for his existence.

To see (perceive) this world we depend on light, sound, form (physical appearance), taste, fragrance even to perceive light we need the senses, eyes, ears, nose, tongue, skin and even for them to work properly, we depend on mind, for mind to work we depend of our soul, our real self the atman, that is the only experience which is not dependent on others, even when our body sleeps and we don't experience this physical world we experience I, when our mind also is inactive in deep sleep state, we experience I. The existence of our real self doesn't depend on anything else and that real self is called siddha vastu (that which is already attained.) He is that atman, the brahman which is self-luminous.

# Om siddhidāya namaḥ।

सिद्धिं फलं कर्तृभ्यो स्वाधिकारानुरूपतो ददातीति सिद्धिदः

siddhiṃ phalaṃ kartṛbhyo svādhikārānurūpato dadātīti siddhidaḥ

He who gives the fruit to the doers according to their eligibility and merit is called siddhida.

Only by his will, the fruits of the karma (good and bad deeds) and various sadhanas (mode of worshipping) is attained.

A verse of contemplation of bhairava says siddhidaḥ sādhakānām – he who is the giver of the fruit to the worshippers.

Sadhana also means a method or a mean for obtaining something. When someone tries to obtain something, it is attained only by his grace.

He is the provider of siddhis. The eight great yoga siddhis, the fruit of chanting mantras etc.

# Om siddhisevitāya namaḥ

He who is worshipped and served by the siddhis (great powers) all the great mahasiddhis (great supernatural powers) and minor siddhis, serve him and help his devotees also even without the devotee going and explicitly requesting those siddhi deities.

Siddhis (powers) and Success are his servants and hence he can grant anyone success and siddhis (powers) at his will effortlessly.

He is greater than all the major and minor siddhis and hence they revere him and serve him.

# Om kaṃkālāya namaḥ।

He is one of the forms of lord Shiva who is non-different from bhairava

भस्मालेपित्रिपुण्ड्रं रुचिरमणिलसत्पिन्छकंकालदक्षं
टंकं वामे कराब्जे दधतमभिलसत्सान्द्रसिन्दूरशोभं
शूलं कृष्णमृगास्यलंबितकरं बद्धेन्दुचूडं हरं
वन्दे देवऋषीश्धरैः परिवृतं वैयाघ्रचर्माम्बरं

bhasmālepitripuṇḍram ruciramaṇilasatpinchakaṃkāladakṣam
ṭamkaṃ vāme karābje
dadhatamabhilasatsāndrasindūraśobham
śūlaṃ kṛṣṇamṛugāsyalambitakaram baddhenducūḍam haram
vande devarṣīśvaraiḥ parivṛtaṃ vaiyāghracarmāmbaram

I bow to the hara, he who has applied the tripundra (three horizontal lines mark) with holy ash, he holds the skeleton, axe, trident, black antelope. He who bears a piece on moon on his crest, he who is covered by tiger skin and prayed by gods and sages surrounding him,

# Om kālāśamanāya namaḥ

He who pacifies time and death. He is beyond time and death, the controller of time and death, he saves his devotees from sudden deaths and sometimes extend their life time if he wishes.

He blesses us with the wisdom that our true self is beyond time and death, we are non-dual to supreme god hood.

# Om kalākāṣṭhātanave namaḥ

He who is in the form of smallest fragments of time, kalā kāṣṭhā. We have discussed in the previous name that he is beyond time but he is also in the form of smallest time fragments like kalā and kāṣṭhā (Kāṣṭhā - 5 Kṣaṇa = 6 seconds)

The supreme godhood is the smallest of the small and biggest of the big says the Vedas.

अणोरणीयान् महतो महीयान् आत्मा

- कठोपनिषद्

The atman, brahman is the most subtle and biggest also. Same attribute of his is shown here.

By referring to kalā kāṣṭhā, it is implicitly indicated that the is also the other fragments of time.

# Om kavaye namaḥ ।

क्रान्तदर्शी कविः सर्वदृक् सर्वज्ञः इति

krāntadarśī kaviḥ sarvadṛk sarvajñaḥ iti

He who sees everything, he who knows everything is kavi,

नान्योतोस्ति द्रष्टा- इति बृहदारण्यकोपनिषत्

nānyotosti draṣṭā- iti bṛhadāraṇyakopaniṣat

There is no one else who is the seer. (i.e.) there is no seer different from him.

कविर्मनीषी परिभूरीति श्रुतिः '

kavirmanīṣī paribhūrīti śrutiḥ '

# Om trinetrāya namaḥ ।

त्रीणि सोमसूर्याग्निरूपाणि नेत्राणि यस्य सः

त्रिनेत्रं त्रिगुणाधारं इति श्रुतिः

trīṇi somasūryāgnirūpāṇi netrāṇi yasya saḥ

trinetraṃ triguṇādhāraṃ iti śrutiḥ

He who has the moon, sun and fire as his eyes.

In the vishvaroopa (universal form) of the supreme god, the here primary light sources are his eyes.

# Om bahunetrāya namaḥ ।

He who has many eyes, meaning he who sees from everything and everyone.

He is the one who resides in everyone as the atman and hence he is the one who sees (perceives) through the senses. Once the atman leaves the body, the body doesn't perceive.

He is the one who perceives through the senses. Here all the senses are denoted through the word netra.

Netra means that which leads us (lead us towards the sensory objects and sensory perceptions) are the senses.

Here the word bahu – meaning many also shows his limitless seeing power. We see only the present; he is beyond time and can see the part present and future.

We see and perceive sensory objects which are in a very limited distance. He has no limit he sees everything and everyone at the same time.

When we concentrate on seeing something, we may not see something else in that particular moment, but he can see everything in every moment.

# Om piṃgalalocanāya namaḥ

He who has reddish-brown eyes.

The reddish-brown color signifies anger, power , authority of control of order.

He can destroy all evil by the mere sight of his eyes.

# Om śūlapāṇaye namaḥ ।

He who holds a trident in his hand.

The importance of the Trishula is described in padma purāna

अथ यज्ञात्मको विष्णु: त्रिशूलं मनसाकरोत्
गुणावस्थाग्निकालात्मलोकशक्तित्रयात्मकं

atha yajñātmako viṣṇu: triśūlaṃ manasākarot
guṇāvasthāgnikālātmalokaśaktitrayātmakaṃ

Lord Vishnu who is the embodiment of yagya - sacred
sacrifices created the Trishula with his mind. The three edges
of the Trishoola indicate three gunas (satva- peace purity and
other qualities. Rajas - over-activeness, pride, etc and tamas -
dullness, ignorance etc.) three states (jaagrat - awaken state,
svapna - dream state, sushupti - deep sleep state) three kinds
of sacred fires, three tenses, and three kinds of powers (ichcha
- interest or desire to do, kriya - the action and gyaana - the
knowledge to do)

By telling that he holds the trishoola which is a representation
of above-mentioned qualities, states and powers, it is clear
that the lord is above all these, and he is not bound to these
but he binds them.

Trishula is described as the embodiment of three gunas and
three shaktis in various shivāgamas also.

By telling that he holds thrishula it is proved that the lord
Bhairava has to ownership of and controllership of Māyā

which is made of three gunas and three shaktis.

# Om khadgapāṇaye namaḥ।

He who holds a sword in his hand.

खण्डति भिनत्ति इति खड्गः निस्त्रिंशः सो अस्य पाण्यां अस्तीति खड्गपाणिः

khaṇḍati bhinatti iti khaḍgaḥ nistrimśaḥ so asya pāṇyām astīti khaḍgapāṇiḥ

That which cuts, or breaks in to many is a khadga, he has it in his hand so he is khaḍgapāṇiḥ

# Om kapāline namaḥ

He who has the skull. We know that lord bhairava took off one of the heads of brahma and used his skull as a beggar bowl to put an end to his pride.

Skull is the part inside which the brain is safe, this indicates that bhairava destroys the pride we gain through knowledge and wisdom (vidyaa mada) and takes us towards god realization.

# Om dhūmralocanāya namaḥ।

He who has eyes which have smoky tone. Smoky tone represents tamasa guna which represents destructive power of his, it also represents māyā

# Om abhirave namaḥ।

अभीरुर्भयशून्यत्वादङ्गनारहितोथवा

abhīrurbhayaśūnyatvādaṅganārahitothavā


Bhīru means coward and abhīru refers to one who doesn't have fear.

He has no fear because we only fear what is greater than us and what is unknown to us. He is the greatest and he is the all knower so he is fearless.

Bhīru is a word used to indicate ladies. Here the word doesn't refer to cowardice but a cute fear which soft, lovable and sensitive ladies possess.

Hence, he is a brahmachari and celibacy is one of his qualities, he doesn't have a lady (wife) hence he is abhīru.

# Om bhairavīnāthāya namaḥ।

He who is the consort of Bhairavi. in previous name, we discussed his celibacy. However, it is to be noted that some forms of Bhairava are accompanied by their consorts (shaktis) feminine embodiments of power.

# Om bhūtapāya namaḥ

The root word pa means to 'protect'

Bhūta means the five great elements, the beings.

He who protects the five great elements, he who protects the beings, he who protects the four kinds of bhūtagrāmas..

The root word pa also means to drink,

In the time of great dissolution, the lord drinks everything the beings, the elements and everything else and destroys them and submerges everything into himself, until the new cycle of creation is begun.

# Om yoginīpataye namaḥ

One who is worshipped by the sixty-four yoginis (forms of Shakti), he who is the consort of the sixty-four yoginis in the form of 64 bhairavas.

# Om dhanadāya namaḥ ।

He who  bestows all kinds of wealth upon us. Everything good that we experience is wealth, health, strength, courage, wisdom, food, children, good qualities, success, victory etc. then finally the ultimate liberation. He blesses us with everything.

# Om dhanahāriṇe namaḥ।

He who takes away wealth from us he who blesses us with wealth can also take away the wealth when we misuse it. Taking away can also mean all and any kind of wealth, which was discussed in the previous name.

# Om dhanavate namaḥ

He who is wealthy

He who owns all the wealth.

# Om prītivardhanāya namaḥ।

Prīti – pleasure, joy, gladness, happiness; enjoyment, graciousness, grace, favour, kindness, propitiousness; friendly disposition, liking, friendliness, amity, regard, harmony, affection, love; conciliation

Vardhana – he who develops, he who increases, strengthens, he who bestows prosperity, growth and success.

# Om nāgahārāya namaḥ।

He who has snakes as his necklace and other ornaments.

Even snakes which are venomous becomes his ornaments, everything is a decoration to him, even terrible things, he is the brahman, in which everything resides and everything is a part of it and nothing is different from it.

Even fierce and terrible things become calm and becomes a lovely part of him. Everything is lovely when he resides in it and everything is lovely when  they are with him.

This also shows us when we connect with him somehow and serve him, we are pure and are respected , praised and loved for we serve them, in spite of any kind of demit we possess.

# Om nāgapāśāya namaḥ।

He who has snakes as his lasso. He who has snakes as his weapon. He who has the celestial weapon of nāga pasha.

Everything is a weapon in his hands, everything is an object in his hand and everything works according to his will. That is his natural ability and power. Everything including our own body and soul is his tool. The good, the bad, the fierce the lovely everything is his tool. That nature of his is indicated by this name.

# Om vyomakeśāya namaḥ ।

गङ्गाधारणसमये व्योमवद्विशालजटावलयरूपः केशः अस्येति व्योमकेशः

gaṅgādhāraṇasamaye vyomavadviśālajaṭāvalayarūpaḥ keśaḥ asyeti vyomakeśaḥ

He who spread his long locks of hair  all over the space, so widely when he had to hold the celestial river of gangā in his long locks of hair.

व्योमकस्य ईशः इति वा व्योमकेशः

vyomakasya īśaḥ iti vā vyomakeśaḥ

Vyomaka means ether or space, he who is the lord of the space, ether element is called vyomakeśa

आत्मन आकाशः संभूतः इति तैतरीयोपनिषद्

ātmana ākāśaḥ saṃbhūtaḥ iti taitarīyopaniṣad

Upanishad says from the atman the ether emerged, and from ether , the air, from air, the fire and from fire the water, and from water the earth, so atman is the source of everything, that atman is our real self. atman is non dual to Bhairava hence he is vyomakesha.

# Om kapālabhṛte namaḥ ।

He holds the skull. The story of lord bhairava cutting the head of brahma the creator for punishing his ego and falsehood is popular in the puranas, after cutting one of the heads of brahma. ( brahma had five heads and after bhairava had cut one, he remained with four heads)

This shows us that he guides us and corrects us by punishing us for our pride and ego and blesses us by rectifying our pride and false ego and helps us realize our true self .

Another meaning of kapāla is

क ब्रह्मा तस्य पालः इति कपालो विष्णुः तं अस्त्ररूपेण बिभर्ति इति कपालभृत्

ka brahmā tasya pālaḥ iti kapālo viṣṇuḥ taṃ astrarūpeṇa bibharti iti kapālabhṛt

Brahma is denoted by the letter 'ka'.  Pāla means protector. He who is the protector even to the brahma the creator is called kapāla.

Lord Vishnu (nārāyana) has protected him in various occasions such as when madhu and kaitabha demons attacked him, when the Vedas were stolen from him etc.

Lord Shiva held him as his arrow on the occasion of destroying of the three cities. Bhairava is non-different from shiva, that makes him kapālabhṛt.

# Om kālāya namaḥ।

कलयति सर्वमिति कालः

kalayati sarvamiti kālaḥ

That which affects everything and creates an effect. That which creates (causes) everything and destroys everything

सर्वभूतानां परिणामहेतुः कालः

sarvabhūtānāṃ pariṇāmahetuḥ kālaḥ

That which is the reason of change, alteration, transformation, evolution. Everything happens in time and because of time.

The lord is that time who is the cause of any change. As we say change is the only one is constant. The lord is that constant. Everything destroys or goes away in time but time remains till the end.

# Om kapālamāline namaḥ।

He who wears the garland of skulls. The skulls are the representation of the 51 syllables of Sanskrit which is the base of all mantras. He has that as the garland, that shows us he is the supreme absolute god (para brahman) who is worshipped by all the mantras.

# Om kamanīyāya namaḥ

शङ्करत्वात् कमनीयः

śaṅkaratvāt kamanīyaḥ

kamanīya – he who is to be desired or wished for

He who is desirable; lovely, pleasing, beautiful

He is so desirable because he is the one  who does good to us. He takes us in the path of welfare, what ever he does to us he does it only for our good, whether we realize it or not. Hence he is naturally desirable by us all.

# Om kalānidhaye namaḥ

One who is the treasure of sixty-four art forms.

Geet vidya — art of Singing.

Vadya vidya — art of playing on musical instruments.

Nritya vidya — art of Dancing.

Natya vidya — art of Theatricals.

Alekhya vidya — art of Painting.

Aiseshakacchedya vidya — art of painting the face and body with color

Tandula-kusuma-bali-vikara — art of preparing offerings from rice and flowers.

Pushpastarana — art of making a covering of flowers for a bed.

Dasana-Vasananga-raga — art of applying preparations for cleansing the teeth, cloths and painting the body.

Mani-Bhumika-Karma — art of making the groundwork of jewels.

Sayya-Racana — art of covering the bed.

Udaka-Vadya — art of playing on music in water.

Udaka-Ghata — art of splashing with water.

Citra-Yoga — art of practically applying an admixture of colors.

Malya-Grathana-Vikalpa — art of designing a preparation of wreaths.

Sekharapida-Yojana — art of practically setting the coronet on the head.

Nepathya-Yoga — art of practically dressing in the tiring room.

Karnapatra-Bhanga — art of decorating the tragus of the ear.

Sugandha-Yukti — art of practical application of aromatics.

Bhushana-Yojana — art of applying or setting ornaments.

Aindra-Jala — art of magic.

Kaucumara — a kind of art.

Hasta-Laghava — art of sleight of hand.

Citra-Sakapupa-Bhakshya-Vikara-Kriya — art of preparing varieties of delicious food.

Panaka-Rasa-Ragasava-Yojana — art of practically preparing palatable drinks and tinging draughts with red color.

Suci-Vaya-Karma — art of needleworks and weaving.

Sutra-Krida — art of playing with thread.

Vina-Damuraka-Vadya — art of playing on lute and small drum.

Prahelika — art of making and solving riddles.

Durvacaka-Yoga — art of practicing language difficult to be answered by others.

Pustaka-Vacana — art of reciting books.

Natikakhyayika-Darsana — art of enacting short plays and anecdotes.

Kavya-Samasya-Purana — art of solving enigmatic verses.

Pattika-Vetra-Bana-Vikalpa — art of designing preparation of shield, cane and arrows.

Tarku-Karma — art of spinning by spindle.

Takshana — art of carpentry.

Vastu-Vidya — art of engineering.

Raupya-Ratna-Pariksha — art of testing silver and jewels.

Dhatu-Vada — art of metallurgy.

Mani-Raga Jnana — art of tinging jewels.

Akara Jnana — art of mineralogy.

Vrikshayur-Veda-Yoga — art of practicing medicine or medical treatment, by herbs.

Mesha-Kukkuta-Lavaka-Yuddha-Vidhi — art of knowing the mode of fighting of lambs, cocks and birds.

Suka-Sarika-Prapalana (Pralapana) -- art of maintaining or knowing conversation between male and female cockatoos.

Utsadana — art of healing or cleaning a person with perfumes.

Kesa-Marjana-Kausala — art of combing hair.

Akshara-Mushtika-Kathana — art of talking with fingers.

Dharana-Matrika — art of the use of amulets.

Desa-Bhasha-Jnana — art of knowing provincial dialects.

Nirmiti-Jnana — art of knowing prediction by heavenly voice

Yantra-Matrika — art of mechanics.

Mlecchita-Kutarka-Vikalpa — art of fabricating barbarous or foreign sophistry .

Samvacya — art of conversation.

Manasi Kavya-Kriya — art of composing verse mentally.

Kriya-Vikalpa — art of designing a literary work or a medical remedy.

Chalitaka-Yoga — art of practicing as a builder of shrines called after him.

Abhidhana-Kosha-Cchando-Jnana — art of the use of lexicography and meters.

Vastra-Gopana — art of concealment of cloths.

Dyuta-Visesha — art of knowing specific gambling.

Akarsha-Krida — art of playing with dice or magnet.

Balaka-Kridanaka — art of using children's toys.

Vainayiki Vidya — art of enforcing discipline.

Vaijayiki Vidya — art of gaining victory.

Vaitaliki Vidya — art of awakening master with music at dawn.

# Om trilocanāya namaḥ ।

त्रीणि सूमसूर्याग्निरूपाणि लोचनानि यस्य सः

यद्वा त्रिषु धामसु जाग्रद्स्वप्नसुषुप्त्यवस्थासु विश्वतैजसप्राज्ञभोक्तृरूपेण स्थूलप्रपञ्चवासनामय आनन्दभोग्यरूपेण तत्तद्विषयभोगरूपेण च विद्यमानस्य सर्वस्य लोचनरूपः लोचनवत्प्रकाशकः

trīṇi sūmasūryāgnirūpāṇi locanāni yasya saḥ

yadvā triṣu dhāmasu jāgradsvapnasuṣuptyavasthāsu
viśvataijasaprājñabhoktṛrūpeṇa
sthūlaprapañcavāsanāmaya ānandabhogyarūpeṇa
tattadviṣayabhogarūpeṇa ca vidyamānasya sarvasya
locanarūpaḥ locanavatprakāśakaḥ

Lochana means eye. He who makes everything visible and hence called eyes, what does he make visible ( make us perceive)

In the awaken state he perceives this world by being the vishva. (world) in dream state he dreams, and in deep sleep perceives the 'I' unconsciously prājña being the jeevatma (soul) and he is also the sensory pleasure enjoyed by the jeevatma, so he is both the enjoyer the enjoyment.

He is prakruti, the jeeva and the atman (brahman) which is the foundation of prakruti and jeeva. Only because of his light everything else (nature and jeeva) is bright.

परमेश्वरम् प्रभुं त्रिलोचनम् इति श्रुतिः

parameśvaram prabhuṃ trilocanam iti śrutiḥ

88

# Om jvalannetrāya namaḥ ।

He who has a brightly shining eyes, we have already discussed that his eyes are the three primary light sources and hence they are shiningly bright.

# Om triśikhine namaḥ ।

He who holds the trident. He who has the three important kinds of sacred fire as his possessions

The agnis (sacred fires) are Ahavaneeya, Gārhapatya and dakshināgni , used in sacred sacrifices.

# Om trilokapāya namaḥ

He who protects all the three worlds.

# Om trinetrayatanayāya namaḥ

He who is the son of the three eyed lord. (Shiva)

Netra means one who guides or leads, trinetra means he who guides or leads the three (the three worlds earth, upper planes and lower planes)

Tanaya means descendant, lord bhairava is a descendant of Shiva, the leader of all worlds, and also a part of Shiva and can be understood that he is just another manifestation of Shiva himself.

# Om ḍiṃbhāya namaḥ

He who is in the form of . a new-born child.

He who is like an . a new-born child who has no attachment, no hatred, he who is always happy with his own self, who doesn't have involvement in the mundane life, he who forgives and forgets easily. He who enjoys everything and stays happy.

There is a story that Bhairava appeared as an infant before wrathful mother kāli to calm her down. When she was so angry and lost control bhairava was lying on the ground and crying in the form of an infant.

The motherhood in goddess kāli was awaken, seeing the cute little infant and she started giving him milk from her own breasts. She calmed down and lost her wrath.

# Om śāntāya namaḥ ।

विषयसुखेष्वसंगतया शान्तः

viṣayasukheṣvasaṃgatayā śāntaḥ

He who is not attached to sensory pleasures.

शान्तः सर्वविकारशून्यः

śāntaḥ sarvavikāraśūnyaḥ

śānta he who is free from all kind of changes (vikāra).

Vikāra means change or deviation from ones own natural state.

Any deformation, change (esp. for the worse) of bodily or mental condition, disease, sickness, hurt, injury,

Vikāra also means perturbation, emotion, agitation, passion

Vikāra also means the six changing states of the body.

Jāyate – is born, asti – exists, vardhate – it grows, viparinamate – it encounters changes, ksheeyate – it slowly detoriates, nashyate – it perishes.

(in Sāṃkhya) a production or derivative from Prakṛti (there are 7 Vikāras, viz. बुद्धि, 'intellect', अहं-कार, 'the sense of individuality', and the 5 तन्-मात्रस् q.v.; these are also producers, inasmuch as from them come the 16 Vikāras which are only

94

productions, viz. the 5 महा-भूतानि q.v., and the 11 organs, viz. the 5 बुद्धीन्द्रियाणि or organs of sense, the 5 कर्मेन्द्रियाणि or organs of action, and मनस्, 'the mind'),

निष्कलं निष्क्रियं शान्तं इति श्वेताश्वतरोपनिषदि

niṣkalaṃ niṣkriyaṃ śāntaṃ iti śavetāśvataropaniṣadi

He who is free from form, he who is free from action and he who is free from sensory pleasures – śavetāśvataropaniṣad

# Om śāntajanapriyāya namaḥ।

He who loves the persons who are śānta, (calm and undisturbed) those who do not get agitated.

Other meanings of the word śānta has been discussed in the previous name.

# Om vaṭukāya namaḥ।

वटुः ब्रह्मचारी

vaṭuḥ brahmacārī

Vaṭu means brahmachari, a student learning the Vedas and vedangas following the norms and conduct of brahmacharya. Celibacy, simplicity, eating whatever he gets which is prescribed by the Vedas without considering the taste etc.

The literal meaning of brahmachāri is -  the one who wanders or walks in the brahma (the Vedas)  meaning he who is always immensely into Vedas and leads a Vedic life.

# Om vaṭuveśāya namaḥ।

Not only that he has the inner qualities of the brahmachāri , but also has the external appearance of the brahmachāri (he has yashti, a sacred stick) he wears a kaupina, he has a sacred thread etc.

Though he doesn't require an external appearance, he adapts it to guide us and put us in the right path.

# Om khaṭvāṃgadhārakāya namaḥ।

He who holds a weapon called khatvāṃga which looks like skull on top of a staff. It's a great weapon used in war by bhairava, kāli etc. it's also described as one of the major weapons of Shiva.

It represents human skull and human body, only because the lord in the form of atman is holding it, it is alive. Once he leaves the hold, it is immobile and lifeless.

उक्तस्त एव खट्वाङ्गं शुद्धसत्व प्रवर्तकम् इति आगम वचनं

uktasta eva khaṭvāṅgaṃ śuddhasatva pravartakam iti āgama vacanaṃ

It is said in the agamas that the weapon khaṭvāṅga is that which develops pure sattvic guna.

# Om bhūtādhyakṣāya namaḥ

Bhūta – the beings

adhyakṣa – अधिष्ठाता पालयिता अध्यक्षः

adhiṣṭhātā pālayitā adhyakṣaḥ

He who exercises supervision. He who inspects, he who is an eye witness.

He who supervises the beings, he who inspects their deeds and blesses the fruit. He who leads all the beings under him.

# Om paśupataye namaḥ

The lord of all the beings.

The being (jeevātmaas) are called pashu (cattle) as they are bound by paasha (rope) like cattle is tied tightly with a rope and is bound to it. The jeevas are bound to avidyaa (Ignorance)

The lord of all such beings is called pashupati. Like the owner of the cattle frees the cattle when the right time comes, the lord frees the beings by blessing them with the wisdom of self-realization. He has the limitless unconditional liberty to keep the souls bound and to untie them.

The lordship referred here is not only the ownership upon souls but also the sole responsibility of protecting them, and liberating them in the right time when the soul is qualified to get the wisdom of self-realization. (i.e.) when the soul attains chitta shuddhi (complete purity of mind and intellect.)

# Om bhikṣukāya namaḥ

He who begs, one of the characteristics of brahmacharya is to beg for food and eat and not try to earn or cook food on their own. Because those efforts may deviate the brahmachāri from Vedic study and may also fall in the trap of likes and dislikes. A  beggar never choses so he doesn't have personal like or dislike. To train that mindset this was the ancient practice followed.

# Om paricārakāya namaḥ

An assistant, a servant, attendant, guard

परितः चरति तस्मात् परिचरकोच्यते

paritaḥ carati tasmāt paricarakocyate

He wanders everywhere completely and guards the world and administers it.

He wanders everywhere when he takes bhiksha (begging)

He is present everywhere and he stays active and hence he is paricaraka

# Om dhūrtāya namaḥ

He who is cunning, crafty, mischievous, he who deceives, he who is a gamester.

Whole world is his play , he is cunning towards evil forces and he deceives them.

We are deceived by the biggest lie that world exist distinctly from brahman. He is the deceiver.

He plays like a mischievous person with his devotees to test them and put them in the right place. He always guides us like a father even while he plays with us his mischiefs of māyā.

# Om digambarāya namaḥ।

He who is naked.

He who has the directions as his clothes, garment,

Since he is spread over everything and everyone, there is nothing different from him which exists there is to cover him up and hence he is naked.  Even if he wears a cloth in in appearance or form , that cloth is also not distinct from him.

He spreads in and beyond the directions so if you want to assume a cloth to the all-pervading and omnipresent god, only directions can be visualized as his dress.


He who covers the directions too with his presence is called digambara. He who covers all the directions by pervading in them.

When we see him in his universal form, the primary light sources are his eyes, the universal wind is his breath and so on, and in that order, direction is his dress.

# Om śūrāya namaḥ

विक्रमणात् शूरः

युद्धे धैर्यवान् शूरः जगत्संहारसमर्थो वा

vikramaṇāt śūraḥ

yuddhe dhairyavān śūraḥ jagatsaṃhārasamartho vā

He who is courageous and brave in war, he who has the power of . swallowing, eating all the worlds.

This name is praised in the Vedas

नमः शूरायचेति श्रुतिः

namaḥ śūrāyaceti śrutiḥ

# Om hariṇāya namaḥ।

He who is greenish. He who is always young and prosperous, aging and death cannot touch him, he is always energetic and charming. Green is the color of prosperity and it symbolizes evergreen.

# Om pāṃḍulocanāya namaḥ

पाण्डुराणि श्वेतानि लोचनानि यस्य सः

pāṇḍurāṇi śvetāni locanāni yasya saḥ

He who has white eyes, white represents purity and grace. His glances are gracious and showering us with bliss, purifies us.

# Om praśāṃtāya namaḥ

प्रकर्षेन शान्तः

prakarṣena śāntaḥ

Who is excellently śānta, who is śānta in the highest degree.

He who has the highest level of peace.

# Om śāṃtidāya namaḥ ।

समस्ताविद्यानिवृत्तिः शान्ति सा ब्रह्मैव तां ददातीति शान्तिदः

samastāvidyānivṛttiḥ śānti sā brahmaiva tāṃ dadātīti śāntidaḥ

śānti means the rectification of all ignorance and that is non different to brahman (absolute god) he gives that to his devotees and hence he is śāntidaḥ

रागद्वेषादिनिर्मोक्षलक्षणां शान्तिं ददातीति शान्तिदः

rāgadveṣādinirmokṣalakṣaṇāṃ śāntiṃ dadātīti śāntidaḥ

He who liberates us from sins, sickness, diseases and gives us peace, hence he is  śāntidaḥ

# Om śuddhāya namaḥ।

कालत्रयेऽपि परमार्थतो माया अविद्यादि संबन्धरहितः

शुद्धमपापविद्धं इति श्रुतिः

kālatraye'pi paramārthato māyā avidyādi sambandharahitaḥ

śuddhamapāpaviddhaṃ iti śrutiḥ

He is free from the attachment or the effect of delusion, primal ignorance etc. in all three times (past, present and future.

# Om śaṃkarapriyabāṃdhavāya namaḥ

He who is the favorite relations, kinsman of Shiva, he is only of his chief attendants who is very close to him.

He who is a relation to the ones who love Shiva, (devotees of Shiva)

# Om aṣṭamūrtaye namaḥ

One who takes eight forms and protects the beings.

The eight element forms of lord Shiva are

Bhava - water

Sharva - earth

Rudra - fire

Ugra - air

Bheema - space, ether

Mahaadeva - moon

Eeshaana - sun

Pashupati – soul

There are the forms of eight primordial nature.

The five elements, the mind (represented by the moon), the intellect (represented by the sun), ahankara (the sense of I) – the soul.

# Om nidhīśāya namaḥ ।

He who is the lord of all treasures.

One who commands the nine kinds of big treasures and its deities and blesses his devotees with great wealth.

1.  mahapadma - $10^{37}$

2.  padma - $10^{32}$

3.  shankha – $10^{12}$

4.  makara

5.  kachchhapa

6.  kumuda - $10^{105}$

7.  kunda

8.  nila - $10^{13}$

9.  kharva - $10^{42}$

Each word refers to a treasure worth billion and trillions. I have given the values to some which I have found from various sources.

# Om jñānacakṣuśe namaḥ ।

He who has the eyes which has the ultimate wisdom,

He who has the ultimate wisdom as his eyes.

He blesses us with the same wisdom.

What is ultimate wisdom, it is seeing (perceiving and experiencing) oneself and everything as one and the same supreme absolute god. (brahman)

# Om tapomayāya namaḥ।

तपः सर्वदोषविनिर्मुक्तं स्वयं प्रकाशमानं ब्रह्मेत्यर्थः

tapaḥ sarvadoṣavinirmuktaṃ svayaṃ prakāśamānaṃ
brahmetyarthaḥ

That which is free from all faults, flaws and demerits. That
which is enlightened, self-luminous. The brahman.

He who is made of austerity and penance.

तपसोध्यजायते इति श्रुतिः

tapasodhyajāyate iti śrutiḥ

# Om aṣṭādhārāya namaḥ

He who is the base of the eight. He who is the base to eight, eight-fold forms of nature

The five great elements, mind, intellect and the sense of 'I'

The foundation or the base and the prime reason for the existence of eight-fold nature is the purusha (the universal consciousness) who is beyond nature.

He who is the base even to the eight directions.

He who is the eight ādhāra chakras of yoga.

# Om ṣaḍādhārāya namaḥ

He who is in the form of six ādhāras. The six yogic power centres the yogic chakras.

मूलाधार – mūlādhāra
स्वाधिष्ठान - svādhiṣṭhāna
मणिपूर - maṇipūra
अनाहत - anāhata
विशुद्ध – viśuddha
आज्ञा - ājñā

# Om sarpayuktāya namaḥ|

He who is accompanied by the serpents. Since the previous name was ṣaḍādhāra, we can take this serpent as a representation of kundalini shakti (yogic power) he is the lord of that power and is always accompanied by her.

# Om śikhisakhāya namaḥ

He who is the friend of peacock.

Previous name was he is accompanied by serpents, this name means friend of peacock. That is he is not an enemy of peacock because he is with the snakes and he is not the enemy of the snakes though he is a friend of peacock meaning he treats every being equal. He maintains the balance and preserves the world as the whole.

He who is the friend to fire.

Śikhi means that which has flames , (i.e.) fire.

He is the friend and guide of the fire. He is the one who preserves the sacred fire of ritualistic sacrifice and stops negative forces from causing harm to it.

He who is the friend of a brahmin

He guides  the brahmin to study vedas. He also appears in the brahmin form for this very purpose. He guides them in their right path. He blesses them with the fruit of their austerity. He is the god as well as the guru.

# Om bhūdharāya namaḥ।

भूमिं गिरिरूपेण धरतीति भूधरः  संकर्षणरूपेण व

bhūmiṃ girirūpeṇa dharatīti bhūdharaḥ  saṃkarṣaṇarūpeṇa va

He who holds the earth in the form of mountains

He who holds the earth

He who holds the earth in the form of saṃkarṣaṇa who is non different from rudra.

# Om bhudharādhīśāya namaḥ।

He who is the lord of the mountains. Shiva is called gireesha, lord of the mountains, bhairava is non different to him.

# Om bhūpataye namaḥ

He who is the lord of the earth, the protector of the earth and its commander.

# Om bhūdharātmajāya namaḥ

He who is the son of the one who holds the earth.

Ātmaja means son, he who emerges from the self/ soul of the father.

By that the meaning here is son of the mountain or he who emerged from the mountain.

Pure wisdom emerges from the Himalayas (from the austerity of the sages doing worship and penance in the Himalayas),that is why goddess uma the embodiment of the true wisdom of the self (brahma vidya) is the daughter of Himalayas in the philosophical sense.

Here the bhairava is also worshipped as the same true wisdom of the self.

Brahman in the form of sankarshana (rudra) bears the earth, he who is the son of rudra who bears the earth.

# Om kaṃkāladhāriṇe namaḥ।

कङ्कालं शरीरस्थि तस्य धारयिता अनेन परमेश्वरस्य नित्यत्वं
ब्रह्मादीनामनित्यत्वं च सूचितं

kaṅkālaṃ śarīrasthi tasya dhārayitā anena parameśvarasya
nityatvaṃ brahmādīnāmanityatvaṃ ca sūcitaṃ

He who wears the skeleton. By this the eternal existence of the
lord is emphasized. Even after brahma and other gods die, the
lord Bhairava prevails and he rips of the skeletons of the gods
and other beings who die and wear it as ornaments. This
shows his supremacy and eternal living.

Also, the impermanent nature of others.

# Om muṇḍine namaḥ

He who has the munda, the head,

He who has shaved his head,

He who is a saint

He who is the protector.

Shaving the head is the symbolic representation of detachment from everything, getting separated from the false ego and experiencing the oneness with the supreme absolute godhood (brahman)

# Om nāgayajñopavītavate namaḥ।

He who wears a serpent as the sacred thread. His sacred thread is an indication of his brahmacharya, Vedic austerity and wisdom.

# Om jṛmbhaṇāya namaḥ

He who makes us yawn, he who puts us in to sleep. He is the embodiment of time, he is the one who wakes us up and make us function, he is the one who makes us sleep and gives us rest. Whether be it daily or in the time of dissolution of one cycle of creation, we are rest in him in the form of jeevatmans.

# Om mohanāya namaḥ

He who deludes, stupefies. He puts us in the biggest illusion of mundane life and death circle, until we realize our true self which is beyond body, mind and intellect.

# Om staṃbhine namaḥ

He who can do the acts of stopping, making immovable, hindering, arresting, bringing to a stand, suppression, obstruction

# Om māraṇāya namaḥ

He who kills, slays, destroys, slaughters, he who puts an end to life and gives death.

# Om kṣobhaṇāya namaḥ ।

सर्गकाले प्रकृतिं पुरुषं च प्रविश्य क्षोभयामासेति क्षोभनः

sargakāle prakṛtiṃ puruṣaṃ ca praviśya kṣobhayāmāseti
kṣobhanaḥ

In the time of creation, he enters inside nature and universal consciousness and vibrates it for creation to happen, he inspires both nature and life to preserve and prevail the creation.

# Om śuddhanīlāṃjanaprakhyāya namaḥ ।

He who has the complexion of pure blue-black pigment or collyrium applied to the eye-lashes or the inner coat of the eyelids. We have discussed this complexion of his in some of the Dhyana shlokas in the beginning.

# Om daityaghne namaḥ

He who is the destroyer of demons , evil forces.

# Om muṇḍabhūṣitāya namaḥ।

He who is adorned by the garland of heads. This shows that everyone is temporary and he is eternal, he wears their traces as an ornament.

Every one die in time and their traces remain as memories in time after their death, lord is the embodiment of time and hence this indicates that characteristic of time.

# Om balibhuje namaḥ ।

Bali is an oblation, a gift or religious offering

He who accepts our offerings and enjoys it.

Though he has no desire nor need of anything, he is enjoying bliss of the self but just because of compassion, he accepts our offerings and grants our wishes, he shows signs of happiness in response to our devotion by rectifying our karma and blessing us with a good life and finally wisdom of the self.

He has no compulsion to do such things but  just out of pure compassion which is unconditional he takes what we offer and bless us.  The offering we do to him helps us realize that everything is already his and we offer this by saying 'na mama' – not mine, as a symbol of realization and accepts that everything including ourselves is a tool or toy in his divine hands.

# Om balibhuṅnāthāya namaḥ ।

He who is the lord of all those who accept and enjoy the n oblation, gifts or religious offerings. Meaning, the lord of all he gods who are revered by various oblations.

तैर्नाथ्यते तैर्याच्यते तानुपतपति तेषामीष्टे शाश्तीति वा नाथः

tairnāthyate tairyācyate tānupatapati teṣāmīṣṭe śāśtīti vā nāthaḥ

He is requested by the ones who are worshipped by offering oblations. Even the gods request him and get what they need from him. They pray to him for various reasons , desires, they worship him and respect him, they also accept his orders and be under his control and hence he is the lord of even the gods and goddesses who are worshipped by mortals.

His supremacy is indicated by this name.

# Om bālāya namaḥ

He who has taken the form of a small child / small kid.

# Om abālaparākramāya namaḥ

abāla – that which is not like a child

parākrama - heroism, prowess, valour, courage, power, strength, endeavour

Though he looks like a child (according to the previous name), his prowess is not limited to a kid's power or strength but he has limitless strength and power.

His soft and tender charming appearance should not be used to judge his valour and power. He is tender, soft and terrific, fierce at the same time. Entirely contradicting attributes can only be present in a divine form, he knows well when to show which characteristic of his and when to assume a wrathful form for the welfare of the world.

abālaparākrama means heroism and prowess which is capable of achieving anything and everything he wishes to.

परानभिभवनीयः सर्वभयंकरो पराक्रमः यस्य सः

parānabhibhavanīyaḥ sarvabhayaṃkaro parākramaḥ yasya saḥ

# Om sarvāpattāraṇāya namaḥ

Sarva – all, every

Āpat - misfortune, calamity, distress, unhappy situations, dangers

tāraṇa - who causes or enables to cross; helping over a difficulty. He who saves, liberates

He who helps us cross all kinds of dangers, he who uplifts us from dangers and difficult life situations.

He does that in many levels, he stops the dangers from affecting us in extreme level by pacifying the effect of our karma to a certain extent, he gives us strength to fight with the dangers we earn due to our own karma. He blesses us with the true wisdom of the real self and makes us experience that there is only brahman and nothing else and all the sufferings of the world cannot even touch our real self, atman which is non dual to brahman.

# Om durgāya namaḥ।

अन्तरायप्रतिहतैः दुःखादवाप्यत इति दुर्गः

antarāyapratihataiḥ duḥkhādavāpyata iti durgaḥ

He who cannot be reached or attained easily by the ones who are defeated by obstacles. And impediments.

दुःखेन गन्तुं अवगन्तुं योग्यो दुर्गः

duḥkhena gantum avagantum yogyo durgaḥ

He who cannot be easily understood, one has to put lot of efforts to understand him and he is worthy of such efforts.

# Om duṣṭabhūtaniṣevitāya namaḥ ।

duṣṭabhūta – evil beings, evil ghosts, bad spirits etc.

niṣevita -served by, obeyed by, honored by, attended by, resorted to by

He who is served even by the bad ghosts and spirits. That is because he is the ultimate controller and commander, the good ones love to serve god and willingly do but the bad ones serve him because he over powers them, controls them and regulates them.

The obey them due to his ultimate authority, they have no choice but to obey him and after starting to serve him, they start respecting him and hence they honor him for his power and for his compassion due to which he accepts even these bad spirits. Then slowly they evolve and then they become his attendants. Once they are completely his attendants, the abide by the conduct of the ghanas, they know the dharma, they become his devotee servants.

This shows us that he accepts both good and bad spirits, if he is accepting even ghostly beings who is bad then there is no doubt that if we have bad qualities inside us, even then we can pray to him to take us in to his refuge, and resort to him. He controls us, guides us and regulates us. Slowly remove the bad in us.

# Om kāmine namaḥ

पूर्णकामस्वभावत्वात् कामी

pūrṇakāmasvabhāvatvāt kāmī

He who is desirous. He who has a desire.  What desire does the lord have?

He has the desire to rectify the pain of his devotees and bles him with happiness. He doesn't have desire related to his own happiness are rectification of sorrow because he has no sorrow as he is not attached to anything and he has no wish for joy because he has already attained every desire and there is no desire which is related to him which is left unattained.

Another interpretation is he is praised as desirous because he is always accompanied by extremely beautiful maiden, uma.

Uma is the desire eternal desire of the lord the power of desire - the iccha shakti. He who has that is praised as  kāmin

# Om kalānidhaye namaḥ।

Kalā – energies of sun , moon and fire

nidhiḥ - treasure, treasure house.

Kalas of the sun are called arka kalas.

Kalas are the rays of light which emit from sun moon and fire. All these kalas emerge from the supreme god and only those reflect in the light sources hence he is called the treasure of kalas.

They are twelve in numbers

तपिनी तापिनी धूम्रा मरीची ज्वालिनी रुचिः
सुषुम्ना भोगदा विश्वा बोधिनी धारिणी क्षमा

tapinī tāpinī dhūmrā marīcī jvālinī ruciḥ
suṣumnā bhogadā viśvā bodhinī dhāriṇī kṣamā

Sixteen kalaas of the moon called soma kalaas

अमृता मानदा पूषा तुष्टि पुष्टि रति धृतिः
शशिनी चन्द्रिका कान्ता ज्योत्स्ना श्री
प्रीति अङ्गदा पूर्णा पूर्णामृता

amṛtā mānadā pūṣā tuṣṭi puṣṭi rati dhṛtiḥ
śaśinī candrikā kāntā jyotsnā śrī
prīti aṅgadā pūrṇā pūrṇāmṛtā

The ten kalaas of fire - vahni kalas

धूम्रार्चिरुष्मा ज्वलिनी ज्वालिनी विस्फुलिङ्गिनी ।
सुश्री: सुरूपा कपिला हव्यकव्यवहे अपि ॥

dhūmrārcirusmā jvalinī jvālinī visphulinginī |
suśrī: surūpā kapilā havyakavyavahe api ॥

All these kalās (the embodiment of different kind of light rays) emitting from these three primary light sources, sun, moon and fire. Emerge from lord bhairava (the supreme lord) and he owns these light rays as his treasure. Only because of his grace do sun moon and fire emit light from them.

# Om kāṃtāya namaḥ

अभिरूपतमः कान्तः

abhirūpatamaḥ kāntaḥ

kānta means one who is the most pleasing, handsome, desirable, well-formed and, beautiful.

कस्य ब्रह्मणोप्यन्तः अस्मादिति कान्तः

kasya brahmaṇopyantaḥ asmāditi kāntaḥ

ka means brahma the creator

anta means end.

Even the end of brahma the creator is in his control hence he is called kānta

# Om kāminīvaśakṛde namaḥ

He who has control over the kāminīs.

kāminīs. - desirous, loving, fond, impassioned, affectionate woman

He who controls everything that is desired, or impassioned by the beings.

# Om vaśine namaḥ

He who has self-control over his senses and actions. He who has subdued passions and desires.

# Om sarvasiddhipradāya namaḥ

He who bestows upon us with all kinds of attainments, yogic powers, wisdom etc.

Siddhi in general means success in your doings. He blesses us with all kinds of success in our life

Then kamya siddhi (attainment of desires) is also called siddhi.

Mantra siddhi, attainment of the fruit of practicing and chanting a mantra is called so. Its benefit starts from simple things like help with worldly issues and troubles to attainment of the ultimate wisdom and god realization, self-realization.

Yoga siddhi is the attainment of the ultimate benefit of eight-fold yoga the samAdhi state.

Lord bhairava blesses with all these kinds of minor and major siddhis,

The greatest attainment is the realization of the truth that there is nothing which is to be attained. The self is already the eternal truth which we already experience.

# Om vaidyāya namaḥ।

सर्वविद्यानां वेदितृत्वाद्वैद्यः

sarvavidyānāṃ veditṛtvādvaidyaḥ

वैद्यः तदधीते तद्वेदेत्यप्रत्ययः

vaidyaḥ tadadhīte tadvedetyapratyayaḥ

He who knows it he who has thoroughly studied it is called Vaidya. Meaning he who is dwelling place of all wisdom and knowledge.

Vaidya also means a physician,

ध्यानमात्रेणसर्वरोगोपषमाद्पापोपशमाद्वा (क्लेशोपशमाद्वेति पाठभेदः )

dhyānamātreṇasarvarogopaṣamādpāpopaśamādvā (kleśopaśamādveti pāṭhabhedaḥ )

Just by visualizing him all kinds of diseases are pacified and hence he is called the Vaidya

भिषक्तमं त्वां भिषजां कृणोमि इति श्रुतिः

bhiṣaktamaṃ tvāṃ bhiṣajāṃ kṛṇomi iti śrutiḥ

The Vedas praise him (supreme god)  as the physician

# Om prabhave namaḥ।

सर्वासु क्रियासु सामर्थ्यातिशयात् प्रभुः

sarvāsu kriyāsu sāmarthyātiśayāt prabhuḥ

Since he is capable of doing anything and everything, he is called prabhu. Even those which are magical to the finite are logical to the infinite.

प्रकर्षेण भावनात् प्रभुः

prakarṣeṇa bhāvanāt prabhuḥ

He manifests eminently and in excellence, hence he is prabhu.

# Om viṣṇave namaḥ ।

विवेष्टि व्याप्नोतीति विष्णुः

देशकालवस्तुपरिच्छेदशून्यः इत्यर्थः

vivesṭi vyāpnotīti viṣṇuḥ

deśakālavastuparicchedaśūnyaḥ ityarthaḥ

He is Vishnu because he enters everything and reside in everything, he spreads and pervades,

He who is not limited and bound by time, place or object. He is present everywhere and he is everything in all time and space.

यस्माद् विष्टमिदं सर्वं तस्य शक्त्या महात्मनः
तस्मादेवोच्यते विष्णुः विशेर्धातोःप्रवेशनात्

इति विष्णुपुराणे

yasmād viṣṭamidaṃ sarvaṃ tasya śaktyā mahātmanaḥ
tasmādevocyate viṣṇuḥ viśerdhātoḥpraveśanāt

iti viṣṇupurāṇe

Everything is pervaded by his power and hence he is called Vishnu because the root of the verb 'vish' means to enter.

विष्णुर्विक्रमणात्

viṣṇurvikramaṇāt

He is Vishnu because he strides and pervades

# Phala shruti

अष्टोत्तरशतं नाम्नां भैरवस्य महात्मनः ।
मया ते कथितं देवि रहस्यं सर्वकामदम् ॥ १५॥

aṣṭottaraśatam nāmnām bhairavasya mahātmanaḥ |
mayā te kathitaṃ devi rahasyaṃ sarvakāmadam ॥ 15॥

The hundred and eight names of bhairava the great one has
been told to you by me o goddess, that which is secret and
which is capable of fulfilling all desires.

य इदं पठति स्तोत्रं नामाष्टशतमुत्तमम् ।
न तस्य दुरितं किञ्चिन्न रोगेभ्यो भयं भवेत् ॥ १६॥

ya idaṃ paṭhati stotram nāmāṣṭaśatamuttamam |
na tasya duritaṃ kiñcinna rogebhyo bhayaṃ bhavet ॥ 16॥

Whoever recites this hymn of hundred and eight names which
is the best hymn, he does not get any misfortune, he doesn't
get fear of diseases.

न च मारीभयं किञ्चिन्न च भूतभयं क्वचित् ।
न शत्रुभ्यो भयं किञ्चित्प्राप्नुयान्मानवः क्वचित् ॥ १७॥

na ca mārībhayaṃ kiñcinna ca bhūtabhayaṃ kvacit |
na śatrubhyo bhayaṃ kiñcitprāpnuyānmānavaḥ kvacit ॥ 17॥

one who recites doesn't fear even mass killing diseases, not
fears ghostly forces, or enemies

पातकेभ्यो भयं नैव यः पठेत्स्तोत्रमनुत्तमम् ।
मारीभये राजभये तथा चौराग्निजे भये ॥ १८॥

pātakebhyo bhayaṃ naiva yaḥ paṭhetstotramanuttamam |
mārībhaye rājabhaye tathā caurāgnije bhaye ॥ 18॥

The reciter doesn't have fear from sins. Meaning the reciter is
pure and hence do not commit sins. In times of fear from mass
killing diseases, in time of fear from kings and governments,
in times of fear of robbery or fire.

औत्पातिके महाघोरे तथा दुःखप्रदर्शने ।
बन्धने च तथा घोरे पठेत्स्तोत्रमनुत्तमम् ॥ १९॥

autpātike mahāghore tathā duḥkhapradarśane |
bandhane ca tathā ghore paṭhetstotramanuttamam ॥ 19॥

In times of dangerous calamities,  in times of sorrow or in
times of binding or arrest. One should recite this best hymn.

सर्वं प्रशममायाति भयं भैरवकीर्तनात् ।
एकादशसहस्रं तु पुरश्चरणमुच्यते ॥ २०॥

sarvaṃ praśamamāyāti bhayaṃ bhairavakīrtanāt |
ekādaśasahasraṃ tu puraścaraṇamucyate ॥ 20॥

Every negativity, every danger and fear caused by it pacifies by singing the glory of bhairava. Eleven thousand times, the hymn must be recited for puraścaraṇa.

यस्त्रिसन्ध्यं पठेद्देवि संवत्सरमतन्द्रितः ।
स सिद्धिं प्राप्नुयादिष्टां दुर्लभामपि मानवः ॥ २१ ॥

yastrisandhyaṃ paṭheddevi saṃvatsaramatandritaḥ |
sa siddhiṃ prāpnuyādiṣṭāṃ durlabhāmapi mānavaḥ || 21||

One who recites the hymn three times a day during the time of sandhyaa for one year, attains whatever is desired, even the desires which are too hard to attain.

षण्मासं भूमिकामस्तु जपित्बा प्राप्नुयान्महीम् ।
राजशत्रुविनाशार्थं पठेन्मासाष्टकं पुनः ॥ २२॥

ṣaṇmāsaṃ bhūmikāmastu japitbā prāpnuyānmahīm |
rājaśatruvināśārthaṃ paṭhenmāsāṣṭakaṃ punaḥ || 22||

Whoever recites the hymn for six months with desire to attain lands will attain them,  for the destruction of enemy of the king (enemy of the nation) one should recite the hymn for eight months.

रात्रौ वारत्रयं चैव नाशयत्येव शात्रकान् ।
जपेन्मासत्रयं मर्त्यो राजानं वशमानयेत् ॥ २३॥

rātrau vāratrayaṃ caiva nāśayatyeva śātrakān |
japenmāsatrayaṃ martyo rājānaṃ vaśamānayet || 23||

By reciting three times every night, one can destroy enemies undoubtedly. By reciting it for three months you can bring the king under your control.

धनार्थी च सुतार्थी च दारार्थी चापि मानवः ।
पठेन् (जपेन) मासत्रयं देवि वारमेकं तथा निशि ॥ २४॥

dhanārthī ca sutārthī ca dārārthī cāpi mānavaḥ |
paṭhen (japen) māsatrayaṃ devi vāramekaṃ tathā niśi ॥ 24॥

Any human desiring for wealth, sons and daughters, wife (or husband) should chant the hymn once, every night for three months

धनं पुत्रं तथा दारान्प्राप्नुयान्नात्र संशयः ।
रोगी भयात्प्रमुच्येत बद्धो मुच्येत बन्धनात् ॥ २५॥

dhanaṃ putraṃ tathā dārānprāpnuyānnātra saṃśayaḥ |
rogī bhayātpramucyeta baddho mucyeta bandhanāt ॥ 25॥

Wealth, sons and daughters, wife (or husband) will be attained, without any doubt. Those who are ill frees from fear, those who are bound are freed from bondages

भीतो भयात्प्रमुच्येत देवि सत्यं न संशयः ।
निगडैश्चापि बद्धो यः कारागेहे निपातितः ॥ २६॥

bhīto bhayātpramucyeta devi satyaṃ na saṃśayaḥ |
nigaḍaiścāpi baddho yaḥ kārāgehe nipātitaḥ ॥ 26॥

Those who are affected by fear are freed from fears, o goddess this is the truth, no doubt. Those who are locked with and those who are imprisoned in jail.

शृङ्खलाबन्धनं प्रासं पठेच्चैव दिवानिशि ।
यं यं चिन्तयते कामं तं तं प्राप्नोति निश्चितम् ।
अप्रकाश्यं परं गुह्यं न देयं यस्य कस्यचित् ॥ २७॥

śaṁkhalābandhanaṁ prāptaṁ paṭheccaiva divāniśi |
yaṁ yaṁ cintayate kāmaṁ taṁ taṁ prāpnoti niścitam |
aprakāśyaṁ paraṁ guhyaṁ na deyaṁ yasya kasyacit || 27 ||

.. and tied by chains, should recite the hymn day and night,
(they are freed from it and attain whatever they wish for.

This hymn is greatly secretive in nature, it should not be given
to anyone

सुकुलीनाय शान्ताय ऋजवे दम्भवर्जिते ।
दद्यात्स्तोत्रमिमं पुण्यं सर्वकामफलप्रदम् ॥ २८॥

sukulīnāya śāntāya ṛjave dambhavarjite |
dadyātstotramimaṁ puṇyaṁ sarvakāmaphalapradam || 28 ||

To the one who follows the norms, the one who is calm by
nature, honest, you give this hymn which is purifying in
nature and that which fulfils all desired benefits.

जजाप परमं प्राप्यं भैरवस्य महात्मनः ।
भैरवस्य प्रसन्नाभूत्सर्वलोकमहेश्वरी ॥ २९॥

jajāpa paramaṁ prāpyaṁ bhairavasya mahātmanaḥ |
bhairavasya prasannābhūtsarvalokamaheśvarī || 29 ||

she recited that which is the greatest hymn worthy of reciting of the great Bhairava, and by that she became very happy the mistress of all the worlds.

भैरवस्तु प्रहृष्टोऽभूत्सर्वगः परमेश्वरः ।
जजाप परया भक्त्या सदा सर्वेश्वरेश्वरीम् ॥ ३०॥

bhairavastu prahṛṣṭo'bhūtsarvagaḥ parameśvaraḥ ।
jajāpa parayā bhaktyā sadā sarveśvareśvarīm ॥ 30॥

The Bhairava who is all pervading, omnipresent and the greatest of the lord became so joyous, she recited the hymn (vidyaa) which is the queen of all lords.

# श्रीबटुकभैरवाष्टोत्तरशतनामस्तोत्रम्

आपदुद्धारकबटुकभैरवस्तोत्रम्

॥ श्रीगणेशाय नमः ॥

॥ श्रीउमामहेश्वराभ्यां नमः ॥

॥ श्रीगुरवे नमः ॥

॥ श्रीभैरवाय नमः ॥

मेरुपृष्ठे सुखासीनं देवदेवं त्रिलोचनम् ।
शङ्करं परिपप्रच्छ पार्वती परमेश्वरम् ॥ १॥

श्रीपार्वत्युवाच -
भगवन्सर्वधर्मज्ञ सर्वशास्त्रागमादिषु ।
आपदुद्धारणं मन्त्रं सर्वसिद्धिकरं परम् ॥ २॥

सर्वेषां चैव भूतानां हितार्थं वाञ्छितं मया ।
विशेषमतस्तु राज्ञां वै शान्तिपुष्टिप्रसाधनम् ॥ ३॥

अङ्गन्यासकरन्यासदेहन्याससमन्वितम् ।
वक्तुमर्हसि देवेश मम हर्षविवर्द्धनम् ॥ ४॥

शङ्कर उवाच -
शृणु देवि महामन्त्रमापदुद्धारहेतुकम् ।
सर्वदुःखप्रशमनं सर्वशत्रुविनाशनम् ॥ ५॥

अपस्मारादि रोगानां ज्वरादीनां विशेषतः ।
नाशनं स्मृतिमात्रेण मन्त्रराजमिमं प्रिये ॥ ६॥

ग्रहरोगत्राणनां च नाशनं सुखवर्द्धनम् ।
स्नेहाद्वक्ष्यामि तं मन्त्रं सर्वसारमिमं प्रिये ॥ ७॥

सर्वकामार्थदं पुण्यं राज्यं भोगप्रदं नृणाम् ।
आपदुद्धारणमिति मन्त्रं वक्ष्याम्यशेषतः ॥ ८॥

प्रणवं पूर्वमुद्धृत्य देवी प्रणवमुद्धरेत् ।
बटुकायेति वै पश्चादापदुद्धारणाय च ॥ ९॥

कुरु द्वयं ततः पश्चाद्बटुकाय पुनः क्षिपेत् ।
देवी प्रणवमुद्धृत्य मन्त्रोद्धारमिमं प्रिये ॥ १०॥

मन्त्रोद्धारमिदं देवी त्रैलोक्यस्यापि दुर्लभम् ।
ॐ ह्रीं बटुकाय आपदुद्धारणाय कुरु-कुरु बटुकाय ह्रीग् ।
अप्रकाश्यमिमं मन्त्रं सर्वशक्तिसमन्वितम् ॥ ११॥

स्मरणादेव मन्त्रस्य भूतप्रेतपिशाचकाः ।
विद्रवन्त्यतिभीता वै कालरुद्रादिव द्विजाः ॥ १२॥

पठेद्वा पाठयेद्वापि पूजयेद्वापि पुस्तकम् ।
अग्निचौरभयं तस्य ग्रहराजभयं तथा ॥ १३॥

न च मारिभयं किञ्चित्सर्वत्रैव सुखी भवेत् ।
आयुरारोग्यमैश्वर्यं पुत्रपौत्रादि सम्पदः ॥ १४॥

भवन्ति सततं तस्य पुस्तकस्यापि पूजनात् ।

न दारिद्र्यं न दौर्भाग्यं नापदां भयमेव च ॥ १५॥

श्रीपार्वत्युवाच -
य एष भैरवो नाम आपदुद्धारको मतः ।
त्वया च कथितो देव भैरवःकल्पवित्तमः ॥ १६॥

तस्य नाम सहस्राणि अयुतान्यर्बुदानि च ।
सारं समुद्धृत्य तेषां वै नामाष्टशतकं वद ॥ १७॥

यानि सङ्कीर्तयन्मर्त्यः सर्वदुःखविवर्जितः ।
सर्वान्कामानवाप्नोति साधकःसिद्धिमेव च ॥ १८॥

ईश्वर उवाच -
शृणु देवि प्रवक्ष्यामि भैरवस्य महात्मनः ।
आपदुद्धारकस्येदं नामाष्टशतमुत्तमम् ॥ १९॥

सर्वपापहरं पुण्यं सर्वापत्तिविनाशनम् ।
सर्वकामार्थदं देवि साधकानां सुखावहम् ॥ २०॥

सर्वमङ्गलमाङ्गल्यं सर्वोपद्रवनाशनम् ।
आयुष्करं पुष्टिकरं श्रीकरं च यशस्करम् ॥ २१॥

नामाष्टशतकस्यास्य छन्दोऽनुष्टुप् प्रकीर्तितः ।
बृहदारण्यको नाम ऋषिर्देवोऽथ भैरवः ॥ २२॥

लज्जाबीजं बीजमिति बटुकामेति शक्तिकम् ।
प्रणवः कीलकं प्रोक्तमिष्टसिद्धौ नियोजयेत् ॥ २३॥

अष्टबाहुं त्रिनयनमिति बीजं समाहितः ।

शक्तिः ह्रीं कीलकं शेषमिष्टसिद्धौ नियोजयेत् ॥ २४॥

ॐ अस्य श्रीमदापदुद्धारक-बटुकभैरवाष्टोत्तरशतनामस्तोत्रस्य
बृहदारण्यक ऋषिः । अनुष्टुप् छन्दः।
श्रीमदापदुद्धारक-बटुकभैरवो देवता ।
बं बीजम् । ह्रीं वटुकाय इति शक्तिः । प्रणवः कीलकम् ।
ममाभीष्टसिद्ध्यर्थे जपे विनियोगः ॥

॥ ऋष्यादि न्यासः ॥

श्रीबृहदारण्यकऋषये नमः (शिरसि)।
अनुष्टुप् छन्दसे नमः (मुखे)।
श्रीबटुकभैरव देवतायै नमः (हृदये)।
ॐ बं बीजाय नमः (गुह्ये)।
ॐ ह्रीं वटुकायेति शक्तये नमः पादयोः ।
ॐ कीलकाय नमः (नाभौ)।
विनियोगाय नमः सर्वाङ्गे ।
॥ इति ऋष्यादि न्यासः ॥

॥ अथ करन्यासः ॥

ॐ ह्रां वां ईशानाय नमः अङ्गुष्ठाभ्यां नमः ।
ॐ ह्रीं वीं तत्पुरुषाय नमः तर्जनीभ्यां नमः ।
ॐ हूं वूं अघोराय नमः मध्यमाभ्यां नमः ।
ॐ हैं वैं वामदेवाय नमः अनामिकाभ्यां नमः ।
ॐ हौं वौं सद्योजाताय नमः कनिष्ठिकाभ्यां वमः ।
ॐ ह्रः वः पञ्चवक्त्राय महादेवाय नमः करतलकरपृष्ठाभ्यां नमः ।
॥ इति करन्यासः ॥

॥ अथ हृदयादि न्यासः ॥

ॐ ह्रां वां ईशानाय नमः हृदयाय नमः ।
ॐ ह्रीं वीं तत्पुरुषाय नमः शिरसे स्वाहा ।
ॐ ह्रूं वूं अघोराय नमः शिखायै वषट् ।
ॐ ह्रैं वैं वामदेवाय नमः कवचाय हुम् ।
ॐ ह्रौं वौं सद्योजाताय नमः नेत्रत्रयाय वौषट् ।
ॐ ह्रः वः पञ्चवक्त्राय महादेवाय नमः अस्त्राय फट् ।
॥ इति हृदयादि न्यासः ॥

अथ देहन्यासः ।
भैरवं मूर्ध्नि विन्यस्य ललाटे भीमदर्शनम् ।
नेत्रयोर्भूतहननं सारमेयानुगं भ्रुवोः ॥ २५॥

कर्णयोर्भूतनाथं च प्रेतबाहुं कपोलयोः ।
नासौष्ठयोश्चैव तथा भस्माङ्गं सर्पविभूषणम् ॥ २६॥

अनादिभूतभाष्यौ च शक्तिहस्तखले न्यसेत् ।
स्कन्धयोर्दैत्यशमनं वाहोरतुलतेजसः ॥ २७॥

पाण्योः कपालिनं न्यस्य हृदये मुण्डमालिनम् ।
शान्तं वक्षस्थले न्यस्य स्तनयोः कामचारिणम् ॥ २८॥

उदरे च सदा तुष्टं क्षेत्रेशं पार्श्वयोस्तथा ।
क्षेत्रपालं पृष्ठदेशे क्षेत्रज्ञं नाभिदेशके ॥ २९॥

पापौघनाशनं कट्यां बटुकं लिङ्गदेशके ।
गुदे रक्षाकरं न्यस्येतथोर्वोर्रक्तलोचनम् ॥ ३०॥

164

जानुनोर्घुर्घुरारावं जङ्घयो रक्तपाणिनम् ।
गुल्फयोः पादुकासिद्धं पादपृष्ठे सुरेश्वरम् ॥ ३१॥

आपादमस्तकं चैव आपदुद्धारकं तथा ।
पूर्वे डमरुहस्तं च दक्षिणे दण्डधारिणम् ॥ ३२॥

खड्गहस्ते पश्चिमायां घण्टावादिनमुत्तरे ।
आग्नेय्यामग्निवर्णं च नैरृत्ये च दिगम्बरम् ॥ ३३॥

वायव्यां सर्वभूतस्थमैशान्ये चाष्टसिद्धिदम् ।
ऊर्ध्वं खेचारिणं न्यस्य पाताले रौद्ररूपिणम् ॥ ३४॥

एवं विन्यस्य स्वदेहस्य षडङ्गेषु ततो न्यसेत् ।
रुद्रं मुखोष्ठयोर्न्यस्य तर्जन्योश्च दिवाकरम् ॥ ३५॥

शिवं मध्यमयोर्न्यस्य नासिकायां त्रिशूलिनम् ।
ब्रह्माणं तु कनिष्ठिक्यां स्तनयोस्त्रिपुरान्तकम् ॥ ३६॥

मांसासिनं कराग्रे तु करपृष्ठे दिगम्बरम् ।

अथ नामाङ्गन्यासः ।
हृदये भूतनाथाय आदिनाथाय मूर्द्धनि ॥ ३७॥

आनन्दपादपूर्वाय नाथाय च शिखासु च ।
सिद्धसामरनाथाय कवचं विन्यसेत्ततः ॥ ३८॥

सहजानन्दनाथाय न्यसेन्नेत्रत्रयेषु च ।
परमानन्दनाथाय अस्त्रं चैव प्रयोजयेत् ॥ ३९॥

एवं न्यासविधिं कृत्वा यथावत्तदनन्तरम् ।
तस्य ध्यानं प्रवक्ष्यामि यथा ध्यात्वा पठेन्नरः ॥ ४० ॥

शुद्धस्फटिकसङ्काशं नीलाञ्जनसमप्रभम् ।
अष्टबाहुं त्रिनयनं चतुर्बाहुं द्विबाहुकम् ॥ ४१ ॥

दंष्ट्राकरालवदनं नूपुरारावसङ्कुलम् ।
भुजङ्गमेखलं देवमग्निवर्णं शिरोरुहम् ॥ ४२ ॥

दिगम्बरं कुमारीशं बटुकाख्यं महाबलम् ।
खट्वाङ्गमसिपाशं च शूलं दक्षिणभागतः ॥ ४३ ॥

डमरुं च कपोलं च वरदं भुजगं तथा ।
अग्निवर्णं समोपेतं सारमेयसमन्वितम् ॥ ४४ ॥

ध्यात्वा जपेत्सुसंस्पृष्टः सर्वान्कामानवाप्नुयात् ॥

ध्यात्वा जपेत्सुसंस्पृष्टः सर्वान्कामानवाप्नुयात् ॥

मन्त्रमहार्णवे सात्त्विकध्यानम् -
वन्दे बालं स्फटिकसदृशं कुण्डलोभासिताङ्गं
दिव्याकल्पैर्नवमणिमयैः किङ्किणीनूपुराढ्यैः ॥

दीप्ताकारं विशदवसनं सुप्रसन्नं त्रिनेत्रं
हस्ताग्राभ्याम्बटुकेशं शूलदण्डैर्दधानम् ॥ १ ॥

मन्त्रमहार्णवे राजसध्यानम् -
उद्यद्भास्करसन्निभं त्रिनयनं रक्ताङ्गरागस्रजं
स्मेरास्यं वरदं कपालमभयं शूलं दधानं करैः ॥

नीलग्रीवमुदारभूषणयुतं शीतांशुखण्डोज्ज्वलं
बन्धूकारुणवाससं भयहरं देवं सदा भावये ॥ २॥

मन्त्रमहार्णवे तामसध्यानम् -
ध्यायेन्नीलाद्रिकान्तिं शशिशकलधरं मुण्डमालं महेशं
दिग्वस्त्रं पिङ्गलाक्षं डमरुमथ सृणिं खड्गपाशाभयानि ॥

नागं घण्टां कपालं करसरसिरुहैर्बिभ्रतं भीमदंष्ट्रं,
दिव्याकल्पं त्रिनेत्रं मणिमयविलसत्किङ्किणीनूपुराढ्यम् ॥ ३॥

॥ इति ध्यानत्रयम् ॥

सात्त्विकं ध्यानमाख्यातञ्चतुर्वर्गफलप्रदम् ।
राजसं कार्यशुभदं तामसं शत्रुनाशनम् ॥ १॥

ध्यात्वा जपेत्सुसंहृष्टः सर्वान्कामानवाप्नुयात् ।
आयुरारोग्यमैश्वर्यं सिद्ध्यर्थं विनियोजयेत् ॥ २॥

विनियोगः
ॐ अस्य श्रीबटुकभैरवनामाष्टशतकस्य आपदुद्धारणस्तोमन्त्रस्य,
बृहदारण्यको नाम ऋषिः, श्रीबटुकभैरवो देवता, अनुष्टुप् छन्दः,
ह्रीं बीजम्, बटुकायेति शक्तिः, प्रणवः कीलकं, अभीष्टतां सिद्ध्यर्थं
जपे विनियोगः ॥ ह्रीं ह्रौं नमः शिवाय इति नमस्कार मन्त्रः ॥

॥ अथ ध्यानम् ॥

वन्दे बालं स्फटिकसदृशं कुण्डलोद्धासिवक्त्रं
दिव्याकल्पैरनवमणिमयैः किङ्किणीनूपुराढ्यैः ।

दीप्ताकारं विशदवदनं सुप्रसन्नं त्रिनेत्रं
हस्ताग्राभ्यां वटुकमनिशं शूलदण्डौ दधानम् ॥
करकलितकपालः कुण्डली दण्डपाणिः
तरुणतिमिरनीलो व्यालयज्ञोपवीती ।
क्रतुसमयसपर्याविघ्नविच्छित्तिहेतुः
जयति वटुकनाथः सिद्धिदः साधकानाम् ॥

शुद्धस्फटिकसङ्काशं सहस्रादित्यवर्चसम् ।
नीलजीमूतसङ्काशं नीलाञ्जनसमप्रभम् ॥

अष्टबाहुं त्रिनयनं चतुर्बाहुं द्विबाहुकम् ।
दशबाहुमथोग्रं च दिव्याम्बरपरिग्रहम् ॥

दंष्ट्राकरालवदनं नूपुरारावसङ्कुलम् ।
भुजङ्गमेखलं देवमग्निवर्णं शिरोरुहम् ॥

दिगम्बरमाकुरेशं बटुकाख्यं महाबलम् ।
खट्वाङ्गमसिपाशं च शूलं दक्षिणभागतः ॥

डमरुं च कपालं च वरदं भुजगं तथा ।
आत्मवर्णसमोपेतं सारमेयसमन्वितम् ॥

॥ इति ध्यानम् ॥

॥ मूलमन्त्रः ॥

ॐ ह्रीं बटुकायापदुद्धारणाय कुरु कुरु बटुकाय ह्रीं ॐ

॥ अथ स्तोत्रम् ॥

ॐ ह्रीं भैरवो भूतनाथश्च भूतात्मा भूतभावनः ।
क्षेत्रदः क्षेत्रपालश्च क्षेत्रज्ञः क्षत्रियो विराट् ॥ १॥

श्मशानवासी मांसाशी खर्पराशी स्मरान्तकः ।
रक्तपः पानपः सिद्धः सिद्धिदः सिद्धसेवितः ॥ २॥

कङ्कालः कालशमनः कलाकाष्ठातनुः कविः ।
त्रिनेत्रो बहुनेत्रश्च तथा पिङ्गललोचनः ॥ ३॥

शूलपाणिः खड्गपाणिः कङ्काली धूम्रलोचनः ।
अभीरुर्भैरवीनाथो भूतपो योगिनीपतिः ॥ ४॥

धनदोऽधनहारि च धनवान्प्रीतिवर्धनः । प्रतिभानवान्
नागहारो नागपाशो व्योमकेशो कपालभृत् ॥ ५॥
कालः कपालमाली च कमनीयः कलानिधिः ।
त्रिलोचनो ज्वलन्नेत्रस्त्रिशिखी च त्रिलोकपः ॥ त्रिलोकभृत्
त्रिनेत्रतनयो डिम्भः शान्तः शान्तजनप्रियः ।
बटुको बटुवेशश्च खट्वाङ्गवरधारकः ॥ ७॥

भूताध्यक्षो पशुपतिर्भिक्षुकः परिचारकः ।
धूर्तो दिगम्बरः शूरो हरिणः पाण्डुलोचनः ॥ ८॥

प्रशान्तः शान्तिदः शुद्धः शङ्करप्रियबान्धवः ।
अष्टमूर्तिर्निधीशश्च ज्ञानचक्षुस्तपोमयः ॥ ९॥

अष्टाधारः षडाधारः सर्पयुक्तः शिखीसखः ।
भूधरो भुधराधीशो भूपतिर्भूधरात्मजः ॥ १०॥

कङ्कालधारी मुण्डी च आन्त्रयज्ञोपवीतवान् ।

कपालधारि मुण्डी च नागयज्ञोपवीतवान् ।
जृम्भणो मोहनः स्तम्भी मारणः क्षोभणस्तथा ॥ ११॥

शुद्धनीलाञ्जनप्रख्यो दैत्यहा मुण्डविभूषितः ।
बलिभुग् बलिभुङ्नाथो बालोऽबालपराक्रमः ॥ १२॥

सर्वापत्तारणो दुर्गो दुष्टभूतनिषेवितः ।
कामी कलानिधिः कान्तः कामिनीवशकृद्वशी ॥ १३॥

जगद्रक्षाकरोऽनन्तो मायामन्त्रौषधीमयः ।
सर्वसिद्धिप्रदो वैद्यः प्रभविष्णुरितीव हि ह्रीं ॐ ॥ १४॥

फलश्रुतिः ।
अष्टोत्तरशतं नाम्नां भैरवाय महात्मनः ।
मया ते कथितं देवि रहस्यं सर्वकामदम् ॥ १५॥

य इदं पठति स्तोत्रं नामाष्टशतमुत्तमम् ।
न तस्य दुरितं किञ्चिन्न रोगेभ्यो भयं भवेत् ॥ १६॥

न च मारीभयं किञ्चिन्न च भूतभयं क्वचित् ।
न शत्रुभ्यो भयं किञ्चित्प्राप्नुयान्मानवः क्वचित् ॥ १७॥

पातकेभ्यो भयं नैव यः पठेत्स्तोत्रमुत्तमम् ।
मारीभये राजभये तथा चौराग्निजे भये ॥ १८॥

औत्पत्तिके महाघोरे तथा दुःखप्रदर्शने ।
बन्धने च तथा घोरे पठेत्स्तोत्रमनुत्तमम् ॥ १९॥

सर्वं प्रशममायाति भयं भैरवकीर्तनात् ।

एकादशसहस्रं तु पुरश्चरणमुच्यते ॥ २०॥

यस्त्रिसन्ध्यं पठेद्देवि संवत्सरमतन्द्रितः ।
स सिद्धिं प्राप्नुयादिष्टां दुर्लभामपि मानवः ॥ २१॥

षण्मासं भूमिकामस्तु जपित्बा प्राप्नुयान्महीम् ।
राजशत्र्युविनाशार्थं पठेन्मासाष्टकं पुनः ॥ २२॥

रात्रौ वारत्रयं चैव नाशयत्येव शात्रवान् ।
जपेन्मासत्रयं मर्त्यो राजानं वशमानयेत् ॥ २३॥

धनार्थी च सुतार्थी च दारार्थी चापि मानवः ।
पठेन् (जपेन) मासत्रयं देवि वारमेकं तथा निशि ॥ २४॥

धनं पुत्रं तथा दारान्प्राप्नुयान्नात्र संशयः ।
रोगी भयात्प्रमुच्येत बद्धो मुच्येत बन्धनात् ॥ २५॥

भीतो भयात्प्रमुच्येत देवि सत्यं न संशयः ।
निगडिश्चापि बद्धो यः कारागेहे निपातितः ॥ २६॥

शृङ्खलाबन्धनं प्रासं पठेच्चैव दिवानिशि ।
यं यं चिन्तयते कामं तं तं प्राप्नोति निश्चितम् ।
अप्रकाश्यं परं गुह्यं न देयं यस्य कस्यचित् ॥ २७॥

सुकुलीनाय शान्ताय ऋजवे दम्भवर्जिते ।
दद्यात्स्तोत्रमिमं पुण्यं सर्वकामफलप्रदम् ॥ २८॥

जजाप परमं प्राप्यं भैरवस्य महात्मनः ।
भैरवस्य प्रसन्नाभूत्सर्वलोकमहेश्वरी ॥ २९॥

भैरवस्तु प्रहृष्टोऽभूत्सर्वगः परमेश्वरः ।
जजाप परया भक्त्या सदा सर्वेश्वरेश्वरीम् ॥ ३०॥

॥ इति श्रीबटुकभैरवाष्टोत्तरशतनामस्तोत्रम् सम्पूर्णम् ॥

# śrībaṭukabhairavāṣṭottaraśatan āmastotram

āpaduddhārakabaṭukabhairavastotram

|| śrīgaṇeśāya namaḥ ||

|| śrīumāmaheśvarābhyāṃ namaḥ ||

|| śrīgurave namaḥ ||

|| śrībhairavāya namaḥ ||

merupṛṣṭhe sukhāsīnaṃ devadevaṃ trilocanam |
śaṅkaraṃ paripapraccha pārvatī parameśvaram || 1||

śrīpārvatyuvāca -
bhagavansarvadharmajña sarvaśāstrāgamādiṣu |
āpaduddhāraṇaṃ mantraṃ sarvasiddhikaraṃ param || 2||

sarveṣāṃ caiva bhūtānāṃ hitārthaṃ vāñchitaṃ mayā |
viśeṣamatastu rājñāṃ vai śāntipuṣṭiprasādhanam || 3||

aṅganyāsakaranyāsadehanyāsasamanvitam |
vaktumarhasi deveśa mama harṣavivarddhanam || 4||

śaṅkara uvāca -
śaṛṇu devi mahāmantramāpaduddhārahetukam |
sarvaduḥkhapraśamanaṃ sarvaśatruvināśanam || 5||

apasmārādi rogāṇāṃ jvarādīnāṃ viśeṣataḥ |
nāśanaṃ smṛtimātreṇa mantrarājamimaṃ priye || 6||

graharogatrāṇanāṃ ca nāśanaṃ sukhavarddhanam |
snehādvakṣyāmi taṃ mantraṃ sarvasāramimaṃ priye || 7||

sarvakāmārthadaṃ puṇyaṃ rājyaṃ bhogapradaṃ nṛṇām |
āpaduddhāraṇamiti mantraṃ vakṣyāmyaśeṣataḥ || 8||

praṇavaṃ pūrvamuddhṛtya devī praṇavamuddharet |
baṭukāyeti vai paścādāpaduddhāraṇāya ca || 9||

kuru dvayaṃ tataḥ paścādvaṭukāya punaḥ kṣipet |
devīṃ praṇavamuddhṛtya mantroddhāramimaṃ priye || 10||

mantroddhāramidaṃ devī trailokyasyāpi durlabham |
ॐ hrīṃ baṭukāya āpaduddhāraṇāya kuru-kuru baṭukāya
hrīm |
aprakāśyamimaṃ mantraṃ sarvaśaktisamanvitam || 11||

smaraṇādeva mantrasya bhūtapretapiśācakāḥ |
vidravantyatibhītā vai kālarudrādiva dvijāḥ || 12||

paṭhedvā pāṭhayedvāpi pūjayedvāpi pustakam |
agnicaurabhayaṃ tasya graharājabhayaṃ tathā || 13||

na ca māribhayaṃ kiñcitsarvatraiva sukhī bhavet |

āyurārogyamaiśvaryaṃ putrapautrādi sampadaḥ || 14||

bhavanti satataṃ tasya pustakasyāpi pūjanāt |
na dāridryaṃ na daurbhāgyaṃ nāpadāṃ bhayameva ca ||
15||

śrīpārvatyuvāca -
ya eṣa bhairavo nāma āpaduddhārako mataḥ |
tvayā ca kathito deva bhairavaḥkalpavittamaḥ || 16||

tasya nāma sahasrāṇi ayutānyarbudāni ca |
sāraṃ samuddhṛtya teṣāṃ vai nāmāṣṭaśatakaṃ vada || 17||

yāni saṅkīrtayanmartyaḥ sarvaduḥkhavivarjitaḥ |
sarvānkāmānavāpnoti sādhakaḥsiddhimeva ca || 18||

īśvara uvāca -
śaṛnu devi pravakṣyāmi bhairavasya mahātmanaḥ |
āpaduddhārakasyedaṃ  nāmāṣṭaśatamuttamam || 19||

sarvapāpaharaṃ puṇyaṃ sarvāpattivināśanam |
sarvakāmārthadaṃ devi sādhakānāṃ sukhāvaham || 20||

sarvamaṅgalamāṅgalyaṃ sarvopadravanāśanam |
āyuṣkaraṃ puṣṭikaraṃ śrīkaraṃ ca yaśaskaram || 21||

nāmāṣṭaśatakasyāsya chando'nuṣṭup prakīrtitaḥ |
bṛhadāraṇyako nāma ṛṣirdevo'tha bhairavaḥ || 22||

lajjābījaṃ bījamiti baṭukāmeti śaktikam |
praṇavaḥ kīlakaṃ proktamiṣṭasiddhau niyojayet || 23||

aṣṭabāhuṃ trinayanamiti bījaṃ samāhitaḥ |
śaktiḥ hrīṃ kīlakaṃ śeṣamiṣṭasiddhau niyojayet || 24||

ॐ asya śrīmadāpaduddhāraka-
baṭukabhairavāṣṭottaraśatanāmastotrasya
bṛhadāraṇyaka ṛṣiḥ | anuṣṭup chandaḥ|
śrīmadāpaduddhāraka-baṭukabhairavo devatā |
baṃ bījam | hrīṃ vaṭukāya iti śaktiḥ | praṇavaḥ kīlakam |
mamābhīṣṭasiddhyarthe jape viniyogaḥ ||


|| ṛṣyādi nyāsaḥ ||


śrībṛhadāraṇyakarṣaye namaḥ (śirasi) |
anuṣṭap chandase namaḥ (mukhe) |
śrībaṭukabhairava devatāyai namaḥ (hṛdaye) |
ॐ baṃ bījāya namaḥ (guhye) |
ॐ hrīṃ vaṭukāyeti śaktaye namaḥ pādayoḥ |
ॐ kīlakāya namaḥ (nābhau) |
viniyogāya namaḥ sarvāṅge |
|| iti ṛṣyādi nyāsaḥ ||


|| atha karanyāsaḥ ||


ॐ hrāṃ vāṃ īśānāya namaḥ aṅguṣṭhābhyāṃ namaḥ |
ॐ hrīṃ vīṃ tatpuruṣāya namaḥ tarjanībhyāṃ namaḥ |

ॐ hrūṃ vūṃ aghorāya namaḥ madhyamābhyāṃ namaḥ |

ॐ hraiṃ vaiṃ vāmadevāya namaḥ anāmikābhyāṃ namaḥ |

ॐ hrauṃ vauṃ sadyojātāya namaḥ kaniṣṭhikābhyāṃ vamaḥ |

ॐ hraḥ vaḥ pañcavaktrāya mahādevāya namaḥ

karatalakarapṛṣṭhābhyāṃ namaḥ |

|| iti karanyāsaḥ ||


|| atha hṛdayādi nyāsaḥ ||


ॐ hrāṃ vāṃ īśānāya namaḥ hṛdayāya namaḥ |

ॐ hrīṃ vīṃ tatpuruṣāya namaḥ śirase svāhā |

ॐ hrūṃ vūṃ aghorāya namaḥ śikhāyai vaṣaṭ |

ॐ hraiṃ vaiṃ vāmadevāya namaḥ kavacāya hum |

ॐ hrauṃ vauṃ sadyojātāya namaḥ netratrayāya vauṣaṭ |

ॐ hraḥ vaḥ pañcavaktrāya mahādevāya namaḥ astrāya phaṭ |

|| iti hṛdayādi nyāsaḥ ||


atha dehanyāsaḥ |

bhairavaṃ mūrdhni vinyasya lalāṭe bhīmadarśanam |

netrayorbhūtahananaṃ sārameyānugaṃ bhruvoḥ || 25||


karṇayorbhūtanāthaṃ ca pretabāhuṃ kapolayoḥ |

nāsauṣṭhayościava tathā bhasmāṅgaṃ sarpavibhūṣaṇam || 26||


anādibhūtabhāṣyau ca śaktihastakhale nyaset |

skandhayordaityaśamanaṃ vāhvoratulatejasaḥ || 27||

pāṇyoḥ kapālinaṃ nyasya hṛdaye muṇḍamālinam |
śāntaṃ vakṣasthale nyasya stanayoḥ kāmacāriṇam || 28 ||

udare ca sadā tuṣṭaṃ kṣetreśaṃ pārśvayostathā |
kṣetrapālaṃ pṛṣṭhadeśe kṣetrajñaṃ nābhideśake || 29 ||

pāpaughanāśanaṃ kaṭyāṃ baṭukaṃ liṅgadeśake |
gude rakṣākaraṃ nyasyettathorvorraktalocanam || 30 ||

jānunorghurghurārāvaṃ jaṅghayo raktapāṇinam |
gulphayoḥ pādukāsiddhaṃ pādapṛṣṭhe sureśvaram || 31 ||

āpādamastakaṃ caiva āpaduddhārakaṃ tathā |
pūrve ḍamaruhastaṃ ca dakṣiṇe daṇḍadhāriṇam || 32 ||

khaḍgahaste paścimāyāṃ ghaṇṭāvādinamuttare |
āgneyyāmagnivarṇaṃ ca nairṛtye ca digambaram || 33 ||

vāyavyāṃ sarvabhūtasthamaiśānye cāṣṭasiddhidam |
ūrdhvaṃ khecāriṇaṃ nyasya pātāle raudrarūpiṇam || 34 ||

evaṃ vinyasya svadehasya ṣaḍaṅgeṣu tato nyaset |
rudraṃ mukhoṣṭhayornyasya tarjanyośca divākaram || 35 ||

śivaṃ madhyamayornyasya nāsikāyāṃ triśūlinam |
brahmāṇaṃ tu kaniṣṭhikyāṃ stanayostripurāntakam || 36 ||

māṃsāsinaṃ karāgre tu karapṛṣṭhe digambaram |

atha nāmāṅganyāsaḥ |
hṛdaye bhūtanāthāya ādināthāya mūrddhani || 37||

ānandapādapūrvāya nāthāya ca śikhāsu ca |
siddhasāmaranāthāya kavacaṃ vinyasettataḥ || 38||

sahajānandanāthāya nyasennetratrayeṣu ca |
paramānandanāthāya astraṃ caiva prayojayet || 39||

evaṃ nyāsavidhiṃ kṛtvā yathāvattadanantaram |
tasya dhyānaṃ pravakṣyāmi yathā dhyātvā paṭhennaraḥ ||
40||

śuddhasphaṭikasaṅkāśaṃ nīlāñjanasamaprabham |
aṣṭabāhuṃ trinayanaṃ caturbāhuṃ dvibāhukam || 41||

daṃṣṭrākarālavadanaṃ nūpurārāvasaṅkulam |
bhujaṅgamekhalaṃ devamagnivarṇaṃ śiroruham || 42||

digambaraṃ kumārīśaṃ baṭukākhyaṃ mahābalam |
khaṭvāṅgamasipāśaṃ ca śūlaṃ dakṣiṇabhāgataḥ || 43||

ḍamaruṃ ca kapolaṃ ca varadaṃ bhujagaṃ tathā |
agnivarṇaṃ samopetaṃ sārameyasamanvitam || 44||

dhyātvā japetsusaṃspṛṣṭaḥ sarvānkāmānavāpnuyāt ||

dhyātvā japetsusaṃspṛṣṭaḥ sarvānkāmānavāpnuyāt ||

mantramahārṇave sāttvikadhyānam -
vande bālaṃ sphaṭikasadṛśaṃ kuṇḍalobhāsitāṅgaṃ
divyākalpairnavamaṇimayaiḥ kiṅkiṇīnūpurāḍhyaiḥ ‖

dīptākāraṃ viśadavasanaṃ suprasannaṃ trinetraṃ
hastāgrābhyāmbaṭukeśaṃ śūladaṇḍairdadhānam ‖ 1 ‖

mantramahārṇave rājasadhyānam -
udyadbhāskarasannibhaṃ trinayanaṃ raktāṅgarāgasrajaṃ
smerāsyaṃ varadaṃ kapālamabhayaṃ śūlaṃ dadhānaṃ
karaiḥ ‖

nīlagrīvamudārabhūṣaṇayutaṃ śītāṃśukhaṇḍojjvalaṃ
bandhūkāruṇavāsasaṃ bhayaharaṃ devaṃ sadā bhāvaye ‖
2 ‖

mantramahārṇave tāmasadhyānam -
dhyāyennīlādrikāntiṃ śaśiśakaladharaṃ muṇḍamālaṃ
maheśaṃ
digvastraṃ piṅgalākṣaṃ ḍamarumatha sṛṇiṃ
khaḍgapāśābhayāni ‖

nāgaṃ ghaṇṭāṃ kapālaṃ karasarasiruhairbibhrataṃ
bhīmadaṃṣṭraṃ,
divyākalpaṃ trinetraṃ maṇimayavilasatkiṅkiṇīnūpurāḍhyam
‖ 3 ‖


‖ iti dhyānatrayam ‖


sāttvikaṃ dhyānamākhyātañcaturvargaphalapradam ǀ
rājasaṃ kāryaśubhadaṃ tāmasaṃ śatrunāśanam ‖ 1 ‖

dhyātvā japetsusaṃhṛṣṭaḥ sarvānkāmānavāpnuyāt |
āyurārogyamaiśvaryaṃ siddhyarthaṃ viniyojayet || 2 ||

viniyogaḥ
ॐ asya śrībaṭukabhairavanāmāṣṭaśatakasya
āpaduddhāraṇastomantrasya,
bṛhadāraṇyako nāma ṛṣiḥ, śrībaṭukabhairavo devatā, anuṣṭup
chandaḥ,
hrīṃ bījam, baṭukāyeti śaktiḥ, praṇavaḥ kīlakam, abhīṣṭatāṃ
siddhyirthe
jape viniyogaḥ || hrīṃ hrauṃ namaḥ śivāya iti namaskāra
mantraḥ ||

|| atha dhyānam ||

vande bālaṃ sphaṭikasadṛśaṃ kuṇḍalodbhāsivaktraṃ
divyākalpairnavamaṇimayaiḥ kiṅkiṇīnūpurāḍhyaiḥ |
dīptākāraṃ viśadavadanaṃ suprasannaṃ trinetraṃ
hastāgrābhyāṃ vaṭukamaniśaṃ śūladaṇḍau dadhānam ||
karakalitakapālaḥ kuṇḍalī daṇḍapāṇiḥ
taruṇatimiranīlo vyālayajñopavītī |
kratusamayasaparyāvighnavicchiptihetuḥ
jayati vaṭukanāthaḥ siddhidaḥ sādhakānām ||

śuddhasphaṭikasaṅkāśaṃ sahasrādityavarcasam |
nīlajīmūtasaṅkāśaṃ nīlāñjanasamaprabham ||

aṣṭabāhuṃ trinayanaṃ caturbāhuṃ dvibāhukam |
daśabāhumathograṃ ca divyāmbaraparigraham ||

daṃṣṭrākarālavadanaṃ nūpurārāvasaṅkulam |
bhujaṅgamekhalaṃ devamagnivarṇaṃ śiroruham ||

digambaramākureśaṃ baṭukākhyaṃ mahābalam |
khaṭvāṅgamasipāśaṃ ca śūlaṃ dakṣiṇabhāgataḥ ||

ḍamaruṃ ca kapālaṃ ca varadaṃ bhujagaṃ tathā |
ātmavarṇasamopetaṃ sārameyasamanvitam ||

|| iti dhyānam ||

|| mūlamantraḥ ||

ॐ hrīṃ baṭukāyāpaduddhāraṇāya kuru kuru baṭukāya hrīṃ
ॐ
isakā japa 11 21 51 yā 108 bāra kare

|| atha stotram ||
ॐ hrīṃ bhairavo bhūtanāthaśca bhūtātmā bhūtabhāvanaḥ |
kṣetradaḥ kṣetrapālaśca kṣetrajñaḥ kṣatriyo virāṭ || 1||

śmaśānavāsī māṃsāśī kharparāśī smarāntakaḥ |
raktapaḥ pānapaḥ siddhaḥ siddhidaḥ siddhasevitaḥ || 2||

kaṅkālaḥ kālaśamanaḥ kalākāṣṭhātanuḥ kaviḥ |
trinetro bahunetraśca tathā piṅgalalocanaḥ || 3||

śūlapāṇiḥ khaṅgapāṇiḥ kaṅkālī dhūmralocanaḥ |

abhīrurbhairavīnātho bhūtapo yoginīpatiḥ || 4 ||

dhanado'dhanahāri ca dhanavānprītivardhanaḥ |
pratibhānavān
nāgahāro nāgakeśo vyomakeśo kapālabhṛt || 5 || nāgapāśo
kālaḥ kapālamāli ca kamanīyaḥ kalānidhiḥ |
trilocano jvalannetrastriśikhī ca trilokabhṛt || trilokapaḥ
trinetratanayo ḍimbhaḥ śāntaḥ śāntajanapriyaḥ |
baṭuko baṭuveśaśca khaṭvāṅgavaradhārakaḥ || 7 ||

bhūtādhyakṣo paśupatirbhikṣukaḥ paricārakaḥ |
dhūrto digambaraḥ śūro hariṇaḥ pāṇḍulocanaḥ || 8 ||

praśāntaḥ śāntidaḥ śuddhaḥ śaṅkarapriyabāndhavaḥ |
aṣṭamūrtirnidhīśaśca jñānacakṣustapomayaḥ || 9 ||

aṣṭādhāraḥ ṣaḍādhāraḥ sarpayuktaḥ śikhīsakhaḥ |
bhūdharo bhudharādhīśo bhūpatirbhūdharātmajaḥ || 10 ||

kaṅkāladhārī muṇḍī ca āntrayajñopavītavān |
 var kapāladhāri muṇḍī ca nāgayajñopavītavān |
jṛmbhaṇo mohanaḥ stambhī māraṇaḥ kṣobhaṇastathā || 11 ||

śuddhanīlāñjanaprakhyo daityahā muṇḍavibhūṣitaḥ |
balibhug balibhuṅnātho bālo'bālaparākramaḥ || 12 ||

sarvāpattāraṇo durgo duṣṭabhūtaniṣevitaḥ |
kāmī  kalānidhiḥ kāntaḥ kāminīvaśakṛdvaśī || 13 ||

jagadrakṣākaro'nanto māyāmantrauṣadhīmayaḥ |
sarvasiddhiprado vaidyaḥ prabhaviṣṇuritīva hi hrīṃ oṃ ||
14 ||

phalaśrutiḥ |
aṣṭottaraśataṃ nāmnāṃ bhairavāya mahātmanaḥ |
mayā te kathitaṃ devi rahasyaṃ sarvakāmadam || 15 ||

ya idaṃ paṭhati stotraṃ nāmāṣṭaśatamuttamam |
na tasya duritaṃ kiñcinna rogebhyo bhayaṃ bhavet || 16 ||

na ca mārībhayaṃ kiñcinna ca bhūtabhayaṃ kvacit |
na śatrubhyo bhayaṃ kiñcitprāpnuyānmānavaḥ kvacit || 17 ||

pātakebhyo bhayaṃ naiva yaḥ paṭhetstotramuttamam |
mārībhaye rājabhaye tathā caurāgnije bhaye || 18 ||

autpattike mahāghore tathā duḥkhapradarśane |
bandhane ca tathā ghore paṭhetstotramanuttamam || 19 ||

sarvaṃ praśamamāyāti bhayaṃ bhairavakīrtanāt |
ekādaśasahasraṃ tu puraścaraṇamucyate || 20 ||

yastrisandhyaṃ paṭheddevi saṃvatsaramatandritaḥ |
sa siddhiṃ prāpnuyādiṣṭāṃ durlabhāmapi mānavaḥ || 21 ||

ṣaṇmāsaṃ bhūmikāmastu japitbā prāpnuyānmahīm |

rājaśatryuvināśārtham paṭhenmāsāṣṭakaṃ punaḥ || 22 ||

rātrau vāratrayaṃ caiva  nāśayatyeva śātravān |
japenmāsatrayaṃ martyo rājānaṃ vaśamānayet || 23 ||

dhanārthī ca sutārthī ca dārārthī cāpi mānavaḥ |
paṭhen (japen) māsatrayaṃ devi vāramekaṃ tathā niśi || 24 ||

dhanaṃ putraṃ tathā dārānprāpnuyānnātra saṃśayaḥ |
rogī bhayātpramucyeta baddho mucyeta bandhanāt || 25 ||

bhīto bhayātpramucyeta devi satyaṃ na saṃśayaḥ |
nigaḍiścāpi baddho yaḥ kārāgehe nipātitaḥ || 26 ||

śaṃkhalābandhanaṃ prāptaṃ paṭheccaiva divāniśi |
yaṃ yaṃ cintayate kāmaṃ taṃ taṃ prāpnoti niścitam |
aprakāśyaṃ paraṃ guhyaṃ na deyaṃ yasya kasyacit || 27 ||

sukulīnāya śāntāya ṛjave dambhavarjite |
dadyātstotramimaṃ puṇyaṃ sarvakāmaphalapradam || 28 ||

jajāpa paramaṃ prāpyaṃ bhairavasya mahātmanaḥ |
bhairavasya prasannābhūtsarvalokamaheśvarī || 29 ||

bhairavastu prahṛṣṭo'bhūtsarvagaḥ parameśvaraḥ |
jajāpa parayā bhaktyā sadā sarveśvareśvarīm || 30 ||

|| iti śrībaṭukabhairavāṣṭottaraśatanāmastotram sampūrṇam ||

# Bhairava Ashtottara Shatanamavali – Devanagari Script

ॐ भैरवाय नमः।

ॐ भूतनाथाय नमः।

ॐ भूतात्मने नमः।

ॐ भूतभावनाय नमः।

ॐ क्षेत्रज्ञाय नमः।

ॐ क्षेत्रपालाय नमः।

ॐ क्षेत्रदाय नमः।

ॐ क्षत्रियाय नमः।

ॐ विरजे नमः।

ॐ श्मशानवासिने नमः।

ॐ मांसाशिने नमः।

ॐ खर्पराशिने नमः।

ॐ स्मरांतकाय नमः।

ॐ रक्तपाय नमः।

ॐ पानपाय नमः।

ॐ सिद्धाय नमः।

ॐ सिद्धिदाय नमः।

ॐ सिद्धिसेविताय नमः।

ॐ कंकालाय नमः।

ॐ कालाशमनाय नमः।

ॐ कलाकाष्ठातनवे नमः। नमः।

ॐ कवये नमः।

ॐ त्रिनेत्राय नमः।

ॐ बहुनेत्राय नमः।

ॐ पिंगललोचनाय नमः।

ॐ शूलपाणये नमः।

ॐ खड्गपाणये नमः।
ॐ कंकालिने नमः।
ॐ धूम्रलोचनाय नमः।
ॐ अभिरवे नमः।
ॐ भैरवीनाथाय नमः।
ॐ भूतपाय नमः।
ॐ योगिनीपतये नमः।
ॐ धनदाय नमः।
ॐ धनहारिणे नमः।
ॐ धनवते नमः।
ॐ प्रीतिवर्धनाय नमः।
ॐ नागहाराय नमः।
ॐ नागपाशाय नमः।
ॐ व्योमकेशाय नमः।
ॐ कपालभृते नमः।
ॐ कालाय नमः।
ॐ कपालमालिने नमः।
ॐ कमनीयाय नमः।
ॐ कलानिधये नमः।
ॐ त्रिलोचनाय नमः।
ॐ ज्वलन्नेत्राय नमः।
ॐ त्रिशिखिने नमः।
ॐ त्रिलोकपय नमः।
ॐ त्रिनेत्रयतनयाय नमः।
ॐ डिंभाय नमः
ॐ शान्ताय नमः।
ॐ शान्तजनप्रियाय नमः।
ॐ बटुकाय नमः।
ॐ बटुवेशाय नमः।
ॐ खट्वांगधारकाय नमः।
ॐ भूताध्यक्षाय नमः।

ॐ पशुपतये नमः।
ॐ भिक्षुकाय नमः।
ॐ परिचारकाय नमः।
ॐ धूर्ताय नमः।
ॐ दिगम्बराय नमः।
ॐ शूराय नमः।
ॐ हरिणाय नमः।
ॐ पांडुलोचनाय नमः।
ॐ प्रशांताय नमः।
ॐ शांतिदाय नमः।
ॐ सिद्धाय नमः, ।
ॐ शंकरप्रियबांधवाय नमः।
ॐ अष्टमूर्तये नमः।
ॐ निधीशाय नमः।
ॐ ज्ञानचक्षुशे नमः।
ॐ तपोमयाय नमः।
ॐ अष्टाधाराय नमः।
ॐ षडाधाराय नमः।
ॐ सर्पयुक्ताय नमः।
ॐ शिखिसखाय नमः।
ॐ भूधराय नमः।
ॐ भुधराधीशाय नमः।
ॐ भूपतये नमः।
ॐ भूधरात्मजाय नमः।
ॐ कंकालधारिणे नमः।
ॐ मुण्डिने नमः।
ॐ नागयज्ञोपवीतवते नमः।
ॐ जृम्भणाय नमः।
ॐ मोहनाय नमः।
ॐ स्तंभिने नमः।
ॐ मरणाय नमः।

ॐ क्षोभणाय नमः।

ॐ शुद्धनीलांजनप्रख्याय नमः।

ॐ दैत्यघ्ने नमः।

ॐ मुण्डभूषिताय नमः।

ॐ बलिभुजे नमः।

ॐ बलिभुङ्नाथाय नमः।

ॐ बालाय नमः।

ॐ बालपराक्रमाय नमः।

ॐ सर्वापत्तारणाय नमः।

ॐ दुर्गाय नमः।

ॐ दुष्टभूतनिषेविताय नमः।

ॐ कामिने नमः।

ॐ कलानिधये नमः।

ॐ कांताय नमः।

ॐ कामिनीवशकृते

ॐ वशिने नमः।

ॐ सर्वसिद्धिप्रदाय नमः।

ॐ वैद्याय नमः।

ॐ प्रभवे नमः।

ॐ विष्णवे नमः।

# Bhairava Ashtottara Shatanamavali – English Script

Om  bhairavāya namaḥ ।
Om  bhūtanāthāya namaḥ ।
Om  bhūtātmane namaḥ ।
Om  bhūtabhāvanāya namaḥ ।
Om  kṣetrajñāya namaḥ ।
Om  kṣetrapālāya namaḥ ।
Om  kṣetradāya namaḥ ।
Om  kṣatriyāya namaḥ ।
Om  viraji namaḥ ।
Om  śmaśāna vāsine namaḥ ।
Om  māṃsāśine namaḥ ।
Om  kharvarāśine namaḥ ।
Om  smarāṃtakāya namaḥ ।
Om  raktapāya namaḥ ।
Om  pānapāya namaḥ ।
Om  siddhāya namaḥ ।
Om  siddhidāya namaḥ ।
Om  siddhisevitāya namaḥ ।
Om  kaṃkālāya namaḥ ।
Om  kālāśamanāya namaḥ ।
Om  kalākāṣṭhātanave namaḥ ।
Om  kavaye namaḥ ।
Om  trinetrāya namaḥ ।
Om  bahunetrāya namaḥ ।
Om  piṃgalalocanāya namaḥ ।
Om  śūlapāṇaye namaḥ ।

Om khadgapāṇaye namaḥ ।
Om kaṃkāline namaḥ ।
Om dhūmralocanāya namaḥ ।
Om abhirave namaḥ ।
Om bhairavīnāthāya namaḥ ।
Om bhūtapāya namaḥ ।
Om yoginīpataye namaḥ ।
Om dhanadāya namaḥ ।
Om dhanahāriṇe namaḥ ।
Om dhanavate namaḥ ।
Om prītivardhanāya namaḥ ।
Om nāgahārāya namaḥ ।
Om nāgapāśāya namaḥ ।
Om vyomakeśāya namaḥ ।
Om kapālabhṛte namaḥ ।
Om kālāya namaḥ ।
Om kapālamāline namaḥ ।
Om kamanīyāya namaḥ ।
Om kalānidhaye namaḥ ।
Om trilocanāya namaḥ ।
Om jvalannetrāya namaḥ ।
Om triśikhine namaḥ ।
Om trilokapāya namaḥ ।
Om trinetrayatanayāya namaḥ ।
Om ḍimbhāya namaḥ
Om śāntāya namaḥ ।
Om śāntajanapriyāya namaḥ ।
Om baṭukāya namaḥ ।
Om baṭuveśāya namaḥ ।
Om khaṭvāṃgadhārakāya namaḥ ।
Om bhūtādhyakṣāya namaḥ ।

Om  paśupataye namaḥ।
Om  bhikṣukāya namaḥ।
Om  paricārakāya namaḥ।
Om  dhūrtāya namaḥ।
Om  digambarāya namaḥ।
Om  śūrāya namaḥ।
Om  hariṇāya namaḥ।
Om  pāṃdulocanāya namaḥ।
Om  praśāṃtāya namaḥ।
Om  śāṃtidāya namaḥ।
Om  siddhāya namaḥ,।
Om  śaṃkarapriyabāṃdhavāya namaḥ।
Om  aṣṭamūrtaye namaḥ।
Om  nidhīśāya namaḥ।
Om  jñānacakṣuśe namaḥ।
Om  tapomayāya namaḥ।
Om  aṣṭādhārāya namaḥ।
Om  ṣaḍādhārāya namaḥ।
Om  sarpayuktāya namaḥ।
Om  śikhisakhāya namaḥ।
Om  bhūdharāya namaḥ।
Om  bhudharādhīśāya namaḥ।
Om  bhūpataye namaḥ।
Om  bhūdharātmajāya namaḥ।
Om  kaṃkāladhāriṇe namaḥ।
Om  muṇḍine namaḥ।
Om  nāgayajñopavītavate namaḥ।
Om  jṛmbhaṇāya namaḥ।
Om  mohanāya namaḥ।
Om  staṃbhine namaḥ।
Om  maraṇāya namaḥ।

Om kṣobhaṇāya namaḥ ।
Om śuddhanīlāṁjanaprakhyāya namaḥ ।
Om daityaghne namaḥ ।
Om muṇḍabhūṣitāya namaḥ ।
Om balibhujaṁ namaḥ ।
Om balibhuṅnāthāya namaḥ ।
Om bālāya namaḥ ।
Om bālaparākramāya namaḥ ।
Om sarvāpittāraṇāya namaḥ ।
Om durgāya namaḥ ।
Om duṣṭabhūtaniṣevitāya namaḥ ।
Om kāmine namaḥ ।
Om kalānidhaye namaḥ ।
Om kāṁtāya namaḥ ।
Om kāminīvaśakṛte namaḥ ।
Om vaśine namaḥ ।
Om sarvasiddhipradāya namaḥ ।
Om vaidyāya namaḥ ।
Om prabhave namaḥ ।
Om viṣṇave namaḥ ।

# Contact Me:

You can always feel free to contact me or send me suggestions, doubts to writetokoushik@yahoo.com

Follow me at my blog

Authorkoushik.tumblr.com

# Please Leave a Review

Thank you for reading the book. Hope you enjoyed it.

If you like this book and enjoyed reading, it would be really helpful if you can share your experience by **leaving a review**

If you have had any problems with the book, please feel free to message me through email writetokoushik@yahoo.com

I will try my best to help you with it.


Thank you

Koushik K

# Other Books by Author

Tales of Hanuman

Tales of Hanuman vol 2

Hanuman Chalisa Explained

Hanumad Bhujanga Stotra

Rama Raksha Stotra: A Shield Of Rama's Names

The Heart of Sun God - A Hymn from Valmiki Ramayana

The Names of Sun God - A Hymn From Mahabharata

Surya Dvadashanama Stotra - Twelve Names of Sun God
Shadpadee Stotra - A Hymn on Vishnu by Adi
Shankaracharya

Achyutashtakam: A Hymn on Lord Vishnu by Adi
Shankaracharya

Narayana Kavacham: From Srimad Bhagavata Purana

Pragyavivardana Stotra - A Hymn from Rudrayamalam:
Wisdom Giving Names of Kartikeya Translation
Transliteration and Commentary

Durga Saptashloki - The seven verses from Devi
Mahathmyam (English)

Durga Saptashloki - The seven verses from Devi
Mahathmyam (Tamil)

Durga Chandrakala Stuti: A hymn on Durga by Appayya
Deekshita

The Name of Durga: Durga Nama Anushthana

Sarasvati Ashtottara Shatanama Stotra: Hundred and Eight
Names of Sarasvati

Glories of Shiva: Stories from the Shiva Mahimna Stotra (coming soon)

All books that are published are available through online stores check